How to Hire the Best

How to Hire the Best

The Rural Business Owner's Ultimate Guide to Attracting TOP PERFORMING Employees

Sabrina Starling, PhD, PCC, BCC

Tap the Potential LLC
www.tapthepotential.com

How to Hire the Best:
The Rural Business Owner's Ultimate Guide to Attracting
Top Performing Employees

Sabrina Starling, PhD, PCC, BCC

Published by
Tap the Potential LLC
www.tapthepotential.com
(318) 264-8644
(800) 975-9440 ext. 725

ISBN: 978-0-9980062-0-8
Library of Congress Control Number: 2016934453
1) Business 2) Consulting

Cover Design: Julie Cornia with Black Dog Design LLC
Interior Design: Anne Austin Design

Copyright © 2016 by Dr. Sabrina Starling
First Edition, 2016
Published in the USA

This book is dedicated to my clients who have been so generous in sharing your experiences with me.

I am honored to be included on your journey, sharing in the joys of your WINS as you overcome one challenge after another.

This book is for you.
You are leading the way as *Employers of Choice* in your communities.

Foreword

One fall day a few years ago, I got an email out of the blue from Dr. Sabrina. She'd read *The Pumpkin Plan* and was so moved by the impact it could have for her clients, she requested a bulk order to give every single one a copy of the book for Christmas *(Of course I emailed back right away— after dabbing the drool off my face —what author can resist a bulk order?!)*. Within the year, we collaborated to put on a Pumpkin Plan Kickstart event for her clients in rural Riverton, WY.

But there was a problem…a big problem. You see, *The Pumpkin Plan* is all about how to grow a colossal business. Dr. Sabrina *(I call her The Doc)* explained that many business owners are reluctant to even consider growing their business. How could this be? This made no sense to me.

Dr. Sabrina drew a deep breath and her voice grew heavy. I could tell something was really troubling her.

"Mike," she said, "It's different here. What works in big cities does not work for these owners in rural areas. It's really frustrating to attend industry conferences and listen to business gurus drop some pearls of wisdom about how to market successfully, or grow your business, then come back to your hometown, try what they suggested, and it lands like a lead balloon. We have to adapt your message to the reality that these business owners live, day in and day out."

But I still didn't get it. "What's different?" I really wanted to understand.

The Doc went on to explain, "You need to understand there is one problem these owners grapple with that just does not go away. Quite honestly, I don't know what to do about it. Maybe you can help—I hope you can help.

These businesses are chronically understaffed. It's hard to find good employees, so these owners are working around the clock filling in the gaps to keep their businesses afloat. They tolerate poor behavior from employees because a 'warm body' is better than nobody. If they fire an employee, it's one more job they will be doing themselves. They are already stretched so thin they are ready to snap. Growth just means ten more jobs these owners will have. Who wants that? No amount of money is worth the employee headaches that come along with growth for these owners."

I could tell The Doc was hoping I had a simple solution to this that we could share with her clients during the Kickstart. But I didn't. However, the more we talked about it, an idea began to evolve . . . in her.

The Doc likes to tackle big challenges, and she doesn't stop until she finds solutions. Shortly after our Kickstart, she set out to write the book with the solution. This is the book you hold in your hands. She didn't have the answer right away, but she had a feeling she knew who did—successful rural business owners. She took the approach that every successful business owner must have at least one or two top performing employees in their business. If they have even one top-performing employee, they must have done something right to attract that employee to their business. She set out to uncover what that "something right" was. Even though each of these owners might not have the whole solution, collectively they hold all the pieces to this complex puzzle.

In short, The Doc did what she does best. She got curious and asked a lot of questions…of a lot of successful rural business owners. From these interviews, the solution emerged into a simple, easy to apply strategy that she shares here. Follow it and you will know exactly what to do to attract the best employees to your rural business.

Over the last couple of years The Doc has shared these strategies with her clients, as she has worked with them to drive profit in their businesses. Now, not only are her clients attracting top performing employees and creating great places to work, but their profits are doubling and tripling in a very short period of time. *(Insider tip: She reveals one of her profit-maximizing strategies in her video at www.tapthepotential.com/moreprofit You'll definitely want to check this out.)*

What The Doc and her team are doing with their clients is highly unusual. Nowhere else will you find the people-savvy strategies Dr. Sabrina teaches, combined with the business acumen and intense profit-focus – she's the rural business owners' best-kept secret. Until now.

—Mike Michalowicz
author of *Profit First* and *The Pumpkin Plan*

Heartfelt Appreciation

This book was written during a particularly challenging time in my life. Fortunately, I am surrounded by the best family, friends, mentors, coaches, colleagues, and clients who helped make this book possible. Thank you to the following individuals, who without your contributions and support, this book would not have been written.

A special thank you to each of the business owners who shared your wisdom and experience with me so that we can help rural business owners solve this very real problem: Mike Bailey, Kari Warberg Block, Dave Coffey, Brad Cutler, Charisa Fox, Mark Hunter, Jeff McMenamy, Chuck Parmely, Ron Parmely, Olivia Prince, Dr. Andrew Sapp and Jeff Warburton.

Donna Leyens and Mike Michalowicz, thank you for your support, encouragement, feedback and advice every step of the way from idea to publication and beyond.

Thank you to my clients for trying out these ideas and showing us they work! I feel such joy for you each time you hire a rock star or fire a "warm body" *(I know, firing an employee is a strange WIN to celebrate, but we get it).*

Mom, thanks for finding almost all of the typos and grammatical errors in this book. You've been doing this for me since elementary school and it is finally paying off!

A special thank you to those rural business owners who took time out of your busy days to provide thoughtful feedback *(a few of you even found typos my Mom missed!)*: Kelly

Albright, Ron Parmely, Billie Anne Grigg, Dave Case, Mark Hunter, Bobby Davis, Nancy Nehl, Holly Cassity, Amanda Henry and Chuck Parmely.

Dona Krebs, I appreciate your patient and supportive help in gathering the interviews for this book, formatting the book, and handling the details of the business so I could focus on writing.

To my coaches, Barb Wade, Travis Lane Jenkins and James Malinchak, who encouraged me to write this book, held me accountable and showed me ways to make the experience more enjoyable and easier than it might have been otherwise – thank you!

To my daughters, thank you for inspiring me to do my best every day and reminding me to savor the little moments along the way.

Introduction

It was 2005 and I needed a career change. I was working as a psychologist in the community mental health center in rural Wyoming and feeling burned out. I wasn't sure what was next; I just knew I couldn't keep doing what I had been doing. That's when I discovered coaching, went through training, quit my job and started my business as a coach.

The majority of my first clients were small business owners. They had two primary problems they wanted my help solving: a lack of work-life balance and employee problems. Although I didn't realize it at the time, these two problems stem from a much more daunting problem—the struggle in rural areas to find and hire top performing employees.

I was struck by how hard working and dedicated my clients were to their business, their families and to their employees, whom many consider family. Time and again, I saw my clients working 60, 70 or more hours per week. I heard them talk of frustrated spouses, kids who missed their Moms and Dads, their disillusionment with the idea of the freedom of owning a business, and their disappointment in themselves when they lost their temper with their employees.

These owners are well-respected community leaders. Yet, they struggled. Many confided in me they longed for a simpler time, when it was just them running the business, without employees. Their business felt like a ball and chain, a weight carried on their shoulders, day after day, night after sleepless night.

I've seen business owners scale back and even close their doors. The problem isn't a lack of business opportunity. The problem is the lack of help in their business. That lack of help costs these business owners dearly—lost opportunity, lost profit, high turnover, their own stress-induced health problems, and relationship problems with their spouse and children, etc. It's too much. Those who scale back or shut their doors do so out of their own self-preservation.

This troubles me greatly. Small businesses drive our national economy. In our rural communities, small businesses are the *heart* of their local economies. When you create one new job in a small business, you are supporting a family in your community. When you create 5 jobs in a small business, you are supporting 5 families in your community. When 1 small business with 10 employees goes out of business, at least 11 families are impacted in a negative way. These are kids my daughters play with. These are neighbors down the street. These are friends at my church. I'm NOT okay with that!

As challenging as this problem is, I knew I could apply my skills as a coach and psychologist to address it. I worked with the top thought leaders in small business, hired my own coaches and interviewed successful rural business owners to uncover their strategies and best practices when it comes to hiring exceptional employees and growing a thriving, profitable rural business.

In these pages, I'll share with you what I've learned from these interviews and my experiences in coaching successful rural small business owners. I'll introduce you to rural small business owners who are making it work, and their businesses are thriving.

Time and again, when I'd reach out to an owner for an interview, they'd say something along the lines of: *"I don't think I have much to offer to help other rural business owners hire great employees. I struggle with this myself."* Most only went along with the interview after I shared the following with them:

"This is a very complex and challenging problem. There are no simple solutions. I believe every business owner holds a piece of wisdom, experience or knowledge that is a clue to the solution. Because you've reached the level of success you have, you know *something* that will help another rural business owner with this issue."

In the pages ahead, I share with you the immense wisdom that poured forth in these interviews.

As you dive in, I want to help you start attracting top performing employees for your small business right away, and make sure you are getting top performance from ALL of your employees. After all, if you're reading this, you need help and you need it now. Go to **www.tapthepotential.com** and grab my *5 Secrets to Exceptional Employee Performance.*

1

Rural Business:
The Joys and Challenges

"I think the extent to which I have any balance at all, any mental balance, is because of being a farm kid and being raised in those isolated rural areas."
—James Earl Jones

Rural American small business owners are in on a secret. Rural living is a high quality lifestyle. Passers-through get hung up on the lack of shopping and restaurants, and other big city cultural opportunities, such as theatre. Yet, there's so much more than meets the eye. Rural living is the perfect antidote to the frenetic, stressful pace of life in bustling, overcrowded cities, where it's possible to live yards away from your neighbor and yet, never hold a conversation.

Here is what a few business owners have to say about the perks of rural living:

> *"The small town, family-oriented, atmosphere is the most attractive thing. People know each other.*

95% of my customers I see over and over again. You don't have to worry. You know your neighbors. They help you and you help them. That's what it's all about." —Mike Bailey, Owner of Bailey Enterprises, Riverton, Wyoming

"I like the relationships. I like when I go to the post office, they know me by name. When I go to the bank, they know me by name. It's friendly. You can count on people." —Charisa Fox, Owner of Fox Family Cleaning in Gillette, Wyoming

"In a small town, in a small office, you have more of a sense of family than you have in a corporate environment, which is an advantage for being a small town business owner." —Brad Cutler, owner of an insurance agency in Green River, Wyoming

Many rural business owners have grown up in the area. They have taken over the family business, or have started a business in their hometown. Others have chosen to move to a rural area for the appealing lifestyle.

In addition to the community-oriented appeal of rural settings, rural business owners enjoy some other significant benefits.

Jeff McMenamy, owner of Teton Therapy PC, recognizes the rural opportunity. *"There's less compe-*

tition and it's easier to reach the people. It's easier to touch a market. There may be only one newspaper or one or two radio stations. In a big market, you've got so many avenues for people to get their information. There are usually fewer services in rural areas. In my field, this presents opportunities to meet more needs," says Jeff.

In spite of the significant advantages rural small business owners enjoy, there is a common problem: the struggle to attract good employees to meet the demand for products or services.

The Problem for Rural Business Owners

Less than one hundred years ago, the majority of Americans lived in rural America. However, since 1980, more than 700 rural counties have lost 10 percent or more of their population.[1]

First, let me clarify what I mean by "rural." Definitions of rural vary. Our focus is on the challenges business owners in low population rural areas experience in finding and hiring exceptional employees.

With the exception of the coast, the Western United States is dominated by low-density rural land where the distance between metropolitan areas is larger and population density is lower.

---

[1] Gillham, Christina. "Doughnut Hole Country" *Newsweek*. October 29, 2009.

Currently, only 1 in 5, Americans live in rural areas. The exodus to cities and suburbs has resulted in a dwindling and aging population in rural America.

The implications of this are significant for rural business owners. Rural business owners are faced with a shortage of skilled labor.

The influx of energy related business in some rural areas contributes to this shortage. There are several other factors contributing to a skilled labor shortage:

- Rural areas now typically consist of a higher percentage of elderly people and children than in urban areas, creating a lower proportion of a working age labor pool.

- Compared to urban areas, in rural areas a higher percentage of residents have a disability and are unavailable to the workforce.

- Educational options are fewer in rural areas than in urban areas. This creates a "brain drain" as many talented young people leave rural areas to go to urban areas for school and upon graduation find employment there. Top talent is enticed to stay in metropolitan areas or lured away from rural America.[2]

---

[2] Carr, Patrick & Kefalas, Maria (2009). *Hollowing Out the Middle: The Rural Brain Drain and What it Means for America*. Beacon Press

- To the frustration of small business owners, rural economic development often means attracting large corporations to rural areas. When large businesses come in, they compete with the small businesses for talent. This, in turn, makes it difficult for a successful small business to expand.

In addition, rural populations are frequently more vulnerable than urban areas to economic downturns because of their dependency on specific industries, such as oil and gas, or agriculture.

"The disadvantage of a rural community is you don't have quite the diversity of applicants to select from," says Brad Cutler.

The number one reason rural business owners get trapped working in their businesses as employees, instead of working on the business to grow it, is that finding good quality people is hard. When owners lack confidence in their employees, or lack employees to do the work, owners jump in and lend a hand working in their businesses…waiting on customers, fixing a computer, changing a tire, installing a window, showing a house, or consulting with clients.

"We have high turnover because of the quality of our work expectations and less people to choose from when hiring. When people come in and they

can't do the jobs to our expectations over a certain amount of time, we have to let them go because it's like paying for somebody just to be there. And we know we're in no position to do that," explains Charisa Fox, Co-Owner of Fox Family Cleaning in Gillette, WY.

"We get a lot of customers who want us because we do good work and we stand behind it. Our challenge has been that when we are booked with work, we often have not had enough employees to counter that demand. I would feel like I am letting customers down if I have to turn them down," Ron Parmely, Co-Owner of Overhead Door of Casper, Wyoming tells me.

When a business owner is working in the business instead of on the business, the business stops growing. A business that relies on the owner doing a large majority of the work is very vulnerable. What happens if the owner is injured and unable to work, or becomes ill for an extended period of time?

Most rural business owners are aware of the threats stemming from a labor shortage. They recognize their very survival is at stake. They are just not sure what can be done about the challenges.

"There's a tendency, especially in these smaller markets, to think that we aren't capable of getting the

kind of people we need. So we end up settling because the employment situation is pretty tight and there are not a lot of employees available.

That ends up causing problems long-term because those less-than-desirable employees have a less-than-desirable impact on the other employees who are trying to do a good job and perform well. They end up being the one bad apple that spoils the whole bushel," says Mike Bailey, owner of Bailey Enterprises, Riverton, WY.

Now, for some good news!

There are some encouraging labor trends in rural America. According to Ben Winchester, research fellow for the University of Minnesota Extension Center for Community Vitality, there actually is a "brain gain" in the form of an influx of 30-49 year olds moving to rural areas. Only 20% of these individuals have had previous contact with the rural community to which they move. The majority are completely new to the community and they move in to the community with their families. They are attracted to rural living due to the slower pace of life, higher perceived safety and security, and lower cost of living. They come with good career potential and strong networks. In fact, each new household added to a rural community is worth about $92,000 per year to the overall economy in that rural area.

Rural business owners stand to benefit by attracting these individuals to work for them. Yet, very few are poised to do so.

The Owners

Meet some of the rural business owners who shared their wisdom with us.

◇◇

MIKE BAILEY OF BAILEY ENTERPRISES

◇◇

Growing the Business after Growing up in the Business

When Mike Bailey, President of Bailey Enterprises, was just twelve years old, he spent his summer days very differently than the typical boy.

Mike spent his days at the gas pumps of his father's 2-bay full-service station, filling cars with gas, checking oil, washing windows and running credit cards using the old manual swipers. He'd then run inside to call the cards in, or verify the cards against a list.

Bailey Enterprises has come a long way since then. Instead of manual swipers for credit cards, much of the business is automated. Mike no longer pumps gas, then runs inside to verify a credit card. Although much of his time and energy is spent on growing the business, Mike still changes tires and deals directly with customers.

Bailey Oil is now a regional petroleum supplier, distributing bulk lubricants and wholesale petroleum to small farms, ranches, construction projects and industry throughout Wyoming and surrounding states. Bailey Enterprises consists of seven convenience stores, two tire and automotive service centers, and three unattended car block fueling sites. Yet, when it comes down to it, Mike explains, "We still base most of what we do on the service we can perform. We're a service-based industry."

Mike attributes the majority of his success to recognizing the challenge rural business owners have in finding and growing a great team of people. Mike sees his employees as key to attaining and keeping customers.

Mike is proud of the team of people he's put together. "To extend my business it takes a lot of good people taking care of our customers. And I guess that's the biggest thing I've gained in this whole thing. We've been very lucky. We've been successful. We've been able to grow. We've expanded our facilities and our locations. To do that took finding great people."

In the pages that follow, Mike shares his insights for building a team who deliver an exceptional customer service experience.

JEFF MCMENAMY OF
THE TETON THERAPY TEAM

*Successfully Attracting Professionals
to Rural Areas*

Jeff McMenamy owns Teton Therapy, a physical and occupational therapy practice with two clinics strategically located in rural Fremont County, Wyoming and a new clinic in Cheyenne, WY. His business provides physical and occupational therapy to all different types of diagnoses from infants to geriatrics.

Jeff has grown his business with employee team involvement. Jeff believes every single employee and his or her input is just as important as the next. He involves his team with the toughest business decisions. Jeff says, *"Sometimes my team makes gutsier calls than I would have. They set goals higher than I would have and I am proud of that."*

Teton Therapy has grown from 75 visits a week to well over 354 visits per week, and continues to break its own records. The business is numbers driven, tracking metrics to measure success.

Jeff attributes his success to his team philosophies that are designed to attract and keep the best employees. He stresses to them that they are the face of the company even when they are on their own time in the community.

"One of the challenges of recruiting for a small business in the rural area is you often need to go outside your area to find people. People frequently have little or no idea what your area is like or what there is to offer," Jeff shares.

Coming up, Jeff will be sharing his strategies for successfully attracting professionals to rural areas.

◇◇

◇◇

JEFF WARBURTON OF THE DOUBLE H BAR
◇◇

Staffing Up Quickly to Meet Seasonal Demand

"I was not raised here but was hired as a college student for summers to come up here and work for five seasons, 25 years ago. I met my wife here, we were married between seasons and came back and worked as a married couple for the company. We were the only employees to ever have a kid up here. Our first child was born before our last season as employees, so he was the mascot. When the family wanted to sell, they called me and we bought it. My brother Chris and I and our wives are partners. This is definitely a family business.

My child is now 22 years old, and he's trying to finish up at Utah State University. He wants to come and be involved and this is what he wants to do for his life, as well."

In the pages ahead, Jeff Warburton, co-owner of The Double H Bar, a recreational outfitting business in Jackson, Wyoming shares strategies for staffing up quickly with top performing employees to meet intense seasonal demand.

◇◇◇

◇◇◇

RON PARMELY OF THE OVERHEAD DOOR COMPANY OF CASPER, WYOMING

◇◇◇

Acting Quickly to Remove Employees Who Are Not a Good Fit

"There is more one-on-one contact with the customer in a rural area. It is more of a personal relationship. A lot of our customers know us by name, know our kids, and our dog. So there is more of a connection with our customers as opposed to a huge city where a customer might buy something from you today, and it might be another 4 years before they need you again," says Ron.

The company was started in 1968 by Ron's father in his garage. In 1988, Ron and his brothers bought out their parents. Currently they have about 21 total employees with several of those being family members.

"I am proudest of our reputation that comes from us being around for a while. People know that we take care of issues. And because of that, we are actually getting preferential requests by some of our customers. And they are even willing to pay a little bit more to use us."

Coming up, Ron shares his perspective on the importance of acting quickly when an employee is not a good fit.

What's Possible...

If up until now, you've believed that attracting top performing employees to your business is nearly impossible because you're in a rural area, I invite you to set that belief aside.

Just imagine...

What's possible when you hire the best employees?

What's possible for you?

What's possible for your business?

2

4 Employee Challenges Facing Rural Business Owners

The shortage of labor presents 4 specific challenges for the rural business owner:

1. Finding Exceptional Employees
2. Hiring Exceptional Employees
3. Tolerating Employee Disengagement
4. Firing too Slowly

Challenge #1:
Finding Exceptional Employees

Rural business owners find it so challenging to find exceptional employees, they often feel compelled to lower their hiring standards. This results in a team of marginal employees who require more management. Time and again, owners have confided in me they spend so much time "managing" employee problems, they long to simplify their business and go back to the days before they had employees. When an owner is questioning his or her ability to lead, the first questions I ask are about the quality of the employees the owner is trying to lead.

When owners spend so much time dealing with marginal to poor employees, they do not have the time or resources to devote to nurturing and attracting exceptional employees. This leads to a vicious cycle of turnover.

"I spend the extra time and effort it takes to find that higher quality employee. This saves money in the long term because I am not constantly training and getting rid of people.

If you can find that better employee who is willing to stay longer, you can spend the effort training them and you get return on your investment as opposed to just continually hiring and training. Even though running short-handed while you look for a quality candidate is challenging, it's better not to settle. Don't settle." —Mike Bailey, Bailey Enterprises

The good news is that you may not need as many employees as you think you need. Many rural business owners actually can operate more profitably with fewer employees. To learn more about how I help rural business owners run more profitably with fewer employees, go to www.tapthe-potential.com/moreprofit

The Cost of Lost Opportunity

"If only we had the people to fill the positions, we could go after and get more of those large contracts. We just don't have the people to fulfill the obligations, so we pass on those and stick with what is do-able with our small team."
—Owner who asked to remain anonymous

Growth opportunities are the reason you are in business! When you fail to take advantage of opportunities, you are setting off a vicious downward spiral. If you have any competition you can be sure they will be ready to take on growth when you are not. Passing on business opportunities can be costly and demoralizing. Difficulty finding the right people with the right skills is the number one reason business owners in rural America struggle to take advantage of growth opportunities.

The cost of missing out on growth opportunities is difficult to measure, and who wants to? Thinking about what you might have made if you double or tripled your profit is depressing.

Challenge #2:
Hiring Exceptional Employees

When you do find that exceptional candidate, you may feel a lot of pressure to attract him or her to work for you. You may find yourself 'selling' the position to the candidate, which can have several negative consequences:

- You may fail to screen and interview appropriately because you are so focused on convincing the candidate to come to work for you.

- Remember, an applicant can have great qualifications, but may not be a good fit for your culture. It is much better to find this out during an interview than after you have hired the employee and spent time and money training the employee.

- Instead of hiring a candidate who is a good fit for the position, you end up hiring based on who was most convinced they want the job.

- When business owners hire a candidate whom they have 'sold,' the employee is in a '1-Up' position and may expect the owner to meet his or her demands going forward.

Jeff McMenamy finds that being interested in candidates is more effective than trying to be interesting. *"There's no sense in telling them about the company unless I know that it's something that really matches what they want.*

I try to gain insight and information about what they want and need rather than telling them all the high points or attractive points of our company or area.

I ask open-ended questions to find out as much as I can about them. Some of the questions I ask include:

- *Can you tell me your list of most important things you're looking for in a job?*

- *What have been some of the disappointments you've had in previous jobs?*

- *Are there any things that are deal breakers when it comes to looking at our company?*

- *What are some of the things that are very important to you outside of work?*

- *What are you most passionate about?*

When I talk about our clinics, I don't hide anything and I touch on the points that might be important to them. If the person is not going to be a good fit, I stop the interview."

The Costs of Hiring the Wrong Person

The typical business owner using traditional hiring practices (i.e., posting an ad, collecting resumes, interviewing and checking references) will mis-hire 75% of the time.[3]

Mis-hiring is costly and time-consuming. The U.S. Department of Labor estimates that hiring the wrong entry-level employee costs between $5,000 and $7,000 after three months. Mis-hiring a supervisor that makes $20,000 per year will cost you about $40,000. Hire the wrong $100,000/year manager and you could be out between $200-300,000.[4] Add to this a decrease in employee morale, lost business and dissatisfied customers and you've got every business owner's nightmare.

Recruiting expenses, even for a minimum wage job, average around $3,500. Factor in the cost of training, which is estimated at upwards of $1,200/year per employee for a minimum wage job, and the cost is close to $5,000 when you hire the wrong minimum wage employee.[5]

Assessing goodness of fit based on the limited information gathered in the traditional hiring process is challenging. Large corporations have entire Human Resource Departments charged with recruiting and hiring. You're

---

[3] *Topgrading*, 3rd Edition by Dr. Bradford Smart

[4] http://skillstorm.com/insights/workforce-management/the-true-cost-of-mis-hires/2012/08/08/

[5] http://getvoip.com/blog/2013/09/17/rethink-business-expenses-save-20k-year

doing this on your own, while wearing multiple hats in the business. Most small business owners don't come into business with a doctorate in psychology and people are complex. You need some better tools and strategies to increase your success with hiring.

In the chapters that follow, I will provide you with strategies to improve your chances of attracting a great employee who is a good fit for your business culture.

Be patient with yourself. A little effort here goes a long way. If you improve your hiring each time you hire, you will be saving yourself significant amounts of time and money over the years you are in business. The more you hone and refine these skills, your odds of hiring great employees increase even more.

Challenge #3:
Tolerating Employee Disengagement

"People are definitely a company's greatest asset. It doesn't make any difference whether the product is cars or cosmetics. A company is only as good as the people it keeps."— Mary Kay Ash

Rural business owners often tolerate a lot of "bad" employee behavior just to keep some employees around to get some things done. See if this sounds familiar:

You know you're not getting the best out of these employees. They don't go the extra mile for your customers, even though you've had "that talk" repeatedly in staff meetings. Their morale is low, they show up late, leave early and stand around the counter chit-chatting when you can see 20 things they *could* be doing. The truth is, they do just enough to get by. Plus, they often make mistakes that cost you lots of money in re-work. Ouch!

If you are like most small business owners, you watch your bottom line closely. **Payroll is typically one of the largest expenses in a small business.** Your payroll can also be the source of a significant hidden "profit leak"—employee disengagement.

The Cost of Employee Disengagement & Ineffectiveness

For the typical small business owner, the cumulative cost of employee disengagement can range from several hundred thousand dollars to millions of dollars— ANNUALLY.

We tolerate marginal employees because we think we need to…to survive. But, in actuality, this is the slow kiss of death for your business.

Consider that unhappy, disengaged employees spend only 40 percent of their time on task.[6] In other words, they may show up to work 5 days per week, but you are only getting 2 days of work out of them.

The price of keeping disengaged, ineffective employees is high. Most business owners have no idea how high.

Lost productivity costs the U.S. economy $588 billion annually. A recent national study by Dale Carnegie Training placed the number of 'fully engaged' employees at 29%, and 'disengaged' employees at 26% – meaning nearly three-quarters of employees are not fully engaged (i.e., productive).[7] Most companies have as much as 85 percent of their human resources doing just enough to get by and sometimes even less. The average employee is discontented, under-utilized and not actualizing their potential. They also are less likely to be happy, healthy and enjoying a sense of satisfaction and fulfillment.

The Engagement Matrix

Taking an inventory of your present human resources can help you see where you are losing money.

---

[6] Jessica Pryce-Jones. Positive Profits: How happiness at work impacts the bottom-line. Choice volume 11, number 4 pp 27-28. Dec 2013 issue.

[7] http://www.dalecarnegie.com/imap/white_papers/employee_engagement_white_paper/

The Four Quadrants of Engagement & Effectiveness[8]

Employees generally fall into one of four categories regarding their level of engagement and effectiveness. These can be represented in quadrants as labeled:

Engaged & Ineffective (EI)	**Engaged & Effective (EE)**
Disengaged & Effective (DE)	**Disengaged & Ineffective (DI)**

The Engaged & Ineffective Quadrant (EI)
New hires typically fall into this quadrant. New employees are excited and engaged; but usually ineffective. When new employees come on board, they have a lot to learn before

---

[8] Theresa A. Kienast, MCC, CPCC. Engage employees and become a superhero! *Choice,* Vol 10, Number 2

they become effective. New employees are learning their way around the office, who reports to whom and your day to day operations.

New employees generally are excited and motivated to do their best work for you. They just don't know how to do so. New employees are also a great source of new ideas and can give you feedback to improve your current systems. However, they typically don't have the depth of understanding of your industry and your systems to determine the most relevant feedback or ideas to share and/or implement.

While experience is still needed, all that excitement and energy continues into the next quadrant, 'Engaged & Effective (EE)' where energy and innovation really come alive.

The Engaged & Effective (EE) Quadrant

Engaged and effective employees are still excited—AND— they have been around long enough to have a good working sense of the mechanics of the organization. These employees show up with powerful ideas and have the energy to move them forward.

They contribute with discretionary effort that no company could afford to pay for. They surpass expectations and want to create and implement their ideas.

It is ideal to have the majority of your employees in this quadrant. This is where you get high productivity with minimal mistakes. Much leadership training focuses on how to move employees into this quadrant and keep them there.

The Disengaged & Effective (DE) Quadrant

These employees often remain effective enough to get by, but their energy and creativity are gone. The danger of keeping them around is that they can start dragging others from the EE quadrant down with them as they become disengaged and minimally effective.

Employees who start out engaged, but then become disengaged may be coachable, but you need to intervene with them early. Many business owners procrastinate, hoping the employee's lapses are just temporary and the employee will eventually re-engage.

Don't delay! Address issues as they arise. Employee disengagement feeds on itself. Negativity begets more negativity. Discouragement leads to more discouragement. If you don't feel confident in your coaching skills to address these issues, seek the help of a coach who specializes in training small business owners in coaching employees.

The Disengaged & Ineffective (DI) Quadrant

Disengaged and ineffective employees continuously complain, have very low morale, repeatedly make mistakes, and might even be sabotaging company efforts, yet very few will do enough to actually get fired.

Instead, they continue to drain energy and suck the life out of other employees and the company as a whole. These employees will cost you a bundle and can sink your business.

Calculate the Hard Costs

Let's look at your team and consider what disengagement and ineffectiveness may be costing you.

Step 1: Think about each of your employees. Assign each employee to one of the four quadrants.

Engaged & Ineffective (EI) ____ # Employees	Engaged & Effective (EE) ____ # Employees
Disengaged & Effective (DE) ____ # Employees	Disengaged & Ineffective (DI) ____ # Employees

Step 2: Add the numbers in each of the EI, DE, DI quadrants.

#EI + #DE + #DI = _____

This is the number of your employees affected by disengagement and ineffectiveness.

Here's a reference point to help you compare how your business stacks up:

> Typically we see that the largest share of employees are located in the disengaged quadrants.[9] Statistically, throughout almost twenty years of using this tool, most businesses chart about 85-99% of their workforce into the EI, DE, and DI quadrants, leaving 15% or less of their workforce engaged and effective, providing strong value to their customers.

Step 3: What is the average salary of your employees? If your employees are paid wages, what is the average you pay a wage-based employee per year?

Now, add 33% to this amount to account for payroll taxes, insurance, vacation and any other benefits you provide.

Step 4: Take the number of employees affected by disengagement and ineffectiveness (EI, DE, DI) from Step 2 above and multiply that figure by the average salary with benefits.

If your employees are paid wages, take the number of employees affected by disengagement and ineffectiveness (EI, DE, DI) from Step 2 above and multiply that figure by the average you pay a wage-based employee per year.

This is an estimate of the hard cost of disengaged and

---

[9] Theresa A. Kienast, MCC, CPCC. Engage employees and become a superhero! *Choice,* Vol 10, Number 2

ineffective employees to you! Keep in mind, there are also "hidden" costs in employee disengagement and ineffectiveness, including the high cost of turnover, re-work from correcting mistakes, lost business from offending customers, etc.

Example:
As an example, let's examine a business of 20 employees, with an average annual salary of **$35,000.** When 33% is added into the average salary to account for benefits ($35,000 X .33 = $11,550), the average pay per year for each employee is $46,550.

Of those 20 employees, 75% are in the disengaged or ineffective quadrants (being very conservative). 75% of 20 employees is 15 employees.

15 Employees X $46,550 = $698,250 annually.

Disengagement and ineffectiveness is costing this small business $698,250 over the course of one year! I don't know about you, but I don't like losing over half a million dollars annually!

Investing in a solid strategy to maximize the number of employees in the engaged and effective quadrant is just sound business sense.

What is a Happy Employee Really Worth?

Now that we've considered how much employee disengagement is costing you, let's examine the value of a happy employee.

An extensive research program with over 32,000 participants conducted since 2005 by the iOpener Institute for People and Performance at Work concludes that happiness at work drives employee engagement.[10] **A happy employee is a high performing employee.** Employees who are happiest at work:

- Use 1/10 the sick leave of their least happy peers
- Are 6 times more energized
- Express the intent to stay twice as long in their organizations
- Report being "on task" 80 percent of their work week, compared to their unhappy peers who report being "on task" a mere 40 percent of their work week.

"I'm a firm believer that people need to be happy in the job that they're doing. If you're not happy in the job you're doing, you're not going to do a very good job. You're not going to be satisfied at the end of the day, no matter how much money you're making."—Mike Bailey, Bailey Enterprises

---

[10] Jessica Pryce-Jones. Positive Profits: How happiness at work impacts the bottom-line. Choice volume 11, number 4 pp 27-28. Dec 2013 issue.

6 Primary Reasons for Employee Disengagement

Why Does Disengagement Happen?

Most experts blame immediate supervisors for employee disengagement. Certainly a bad boss who yells and belittles employees will lead employees to become ticked off, apathetic and disengaged. However, in my experience, most of the owners with whom I work are not bad bosses. In fact, they care considerably for their employees and yet they still have problems with disengaged employees.

There are 6 primary reasons for employee disengagement:

#1 Employees don't understand their role in the story of serving your 'Ideal Client'.

FACT: Most business owners don't have a compelling story about the "WHY" of their business and how their business serves a need of their Ideal Client and Customer, much less a story that is appealing to their 'Ideal Employee.' When employees buy into "WHY" your business exists, why you are passionate about the customers and clients you serve, and why what the employee does matters, they are much more likely to be engaged. Taking out the trash is no longer just a chore to be done. It becomes a part of the whole story about why what you do matters.

Here are some questions to get you started:

1. Why do you do what you do for your best clients or customers?

2. What are the greatest, most important problems you solve for your best clients or customers?

3. How can each of your employees be a hero in the story of how your business solves these important, urgent problems for your best clients or customers?

Take the time to create your compelling story about why you do what you do for those you serve. Then, make your employees heroes in the story! Tell the story every chance you get, starting with the initial employment interview, and continuing on from there.

Your employees need to know their hero role. Most don't. We all like to be heroes. *Give your employees the chance to be a hero and watch them do their best for your customers!*

#2 Letting too many slackers hang on for too long.

Letting too many slackers hang on for too long drags down morale. Your best people get tired of cleaning up messes made by the slackers. Plus, word gets out. Exceptional employees do not want to work with a bunch of warm bodies. By keeping warm bodies around, you are actually repelling exceptional employees.

Allowing slackers to hang on too long leads to the third underlying cause for employees to become disengaged.

#3 Bad Behaviors by the Boss
(Notice, I did not say "bad bosses.")
Putting up with employees who consistently make mistakes and who do just enough to get by is maddening for even the most patient of bosses. We all have our breaking points.

When bosses lose their patience with bad employee behaviors, at the worst, the boss yells and screams, which not only ticks off the employee he or she is yelling at, but word gets out and morale goes down for everyone. You feel guilty. Your guilt eats at you and makes you even grumpier. It's a vicious cycle.

Long before you lose your cool, something more insidious happens. It's our human nature to notice and focus on problems. Once you see one problem, you see more and more. It becomes much more difficult to acknowledge what your team is doing right. You become a boss 'on patrol,' continually noticing and commenting on mistakes and oversights, feeling like you are always lecturing your team about what they are doing wrong.

A good rule of thumb is to *strive for a 5:1 ratio of positive to negative comments to your employees.* When you get out of balance by focusing more on the problems, rather than what your team is doing right, morale goes down and even the best employees will become disengaged.

#4 *Failing to Delegate*

Failing to delegate will drag down morale. This often occurs because the business owner does not trust the employees he or she has hired to get the job done.

When you have disengaged or ineffective employees, you don't delegate the $10/hour tasks, much less the $100/hour or the $1000/hour tasks, so you never get around to tapping the full potential of your business, doing your $10,000/

hour work. Let's face it, if you—the CEO, the President, the owner—are not doing your genius work, your business is losing money daily.

There is no reason for you to neglect your business by performing activities that do not play to your strengths. Most of us overestimate how well we perform various tasks. The mere fact that we wear multiple hats and have a long list of things to do, means we are not executing ANY of our tasks at the highest level. Performing any tasks that can be delegated, especially those that others probably can even do better, can free your time to focus on your strengths. Removing one activity that is not your strength can make a major difference to your business and attitude.

Delegation creates the mental space you need to innovatively move your business forward. When you effectively delegate and spend the majority of your time doing your genius work, from your strengths, you'll find you don't even have to work 40 hours per week to move your business forward by leaps and bounds.

Effective delegation is key to keeping your employees engaged. Exceptional employees want to feel competent. Competence comes from being continually stretched to take on new responsibilities and mastering new challenges. Don't hesitate to delegate, thinking you are somehow 'protecting' an employee from becoming overwhelmed. Ask your employees to tell you if they are overwhelmed by the responsibilities they are being assigned.

Delegate and support your employees in carrying out their responsibilities. You'll be amazed at what others are capable of accomplishing in your business!

Now, let's examine another reason employees become disengaged. This one is much more subtle and many business owners overlook it.

#5 A Mismatch between the Employee's Immutable Laws and Yours

Many new hires are excited to work for you. They start out engaged, even though they are relatively ineffective because they are still learning the ropes. Once they are trained and have been with you for a while, they are exactly the kind of employee you want—engaged AND effective.

However, some of those who start out excited, then go on to learn the ropes and become top performers, will become disengaged. This has nothing to do with anything you, the boss, has done to them. It's simply due to a conflict between the employee's Immutable Laws[11] and yours. Immutable Laws are your core values, your fundamental, deeply held beliefs, your highest priorities and the organizing principles that guide your actions.

Surprisingly, the most damaging employees to keep around are top performers whose Immutable Laws are not aligned with yours. These employees are poison to your

11 For a thorough discussion of Immutable Laws, read *The Pumpkin Plan* by Mike Michalowicz.

business. Even though they perform well, they demonstrate a very different set of values from yours.

For most rural business owners, this presents quite the dilemma. It's hard enough to find great employees. If you have a top performer, but that employee consistently handles situations in ways that make you cringe, you have a conflict based on Immutable Laws.

What should you do with them? Terminate them. They damage the integrity of your business in the eyes of your other employees and your customers. By keeping them around, you end up sending mixed, confusing messages that drive away your best employees and customers.

Let's say your top salesperson brings in a lot of revenue, but she rolls her eyes at the new initiatives you introduce and the state-of-the-art training you share in weekly meetings. Maybe she tells your customers that some of what you offer is "irrelevant" to their needs. Because of this, she never shares your latest value-adds with customers because she doesn't see the point. Although her sales make a significant contribution to your bottom-line, she fails to bring in additional revenue because she is not leveraging all the tools and training at her disposal. Furthermore, she's a negative influence on other employees, one of whom recently confided in you that she has looked for work elsewhere because she is so troubled by the on-going negativity coming from your top salesperson.

Although it may be tough to let this person go, in the long run you'll be glad you did. Most owners breathe a sigh of relief after letting an employee like this go.

Later, we'll take a deeper dive into understanding Immutable Laws. I'll also offer you some questions to help you identify your Immutable Laws.

Finally, let's examine the sixth reason for employee disengagement.

#6 Failing to Intervene Quickly When a Good Employee Shows the First Sign of Disengagement

When you have a good employee, who typically performs well and makes you proud, yet one day you observe this employee doing something out of character, intervene as quickly as possible.

Here's how to coach this:

1. Get curious, in a nonjudgmental way, about what is going on with this employee.
2. Express your surprise at this sudden change in the employee's behavior.
3. Be curious, not only about the underlying cause, but also what the employee will do to immediately turn it around.
4. Ask how you might support the employee in his or her efforts to turn the situation around.

Too often, owners are inclined to overlook the problem, hoping it will go away. It won't. Chances are, you're seeing the first sign of a more serious problem to develop. Address it quickly and hold the employee accountable for improvement.

Employee disengagement is costly to your bottom-line. Take action to address these 6 underlying causes of employee disengagement and watch your team thrive, while profits soar!

3 Immediate Actions:

1. Systematize your training to move your new hires (i.e., your Engaged & Ineffective employees) to effectiveness as quickly as possible.

2. Set strong accountability expectations for each position and let those disengaged, ineffective employees know about the accountability expectations. Track progress. They will likely look for work elsewhere soon. If not, encourage them to find work that is a better fit for them and let them go.

3. Attempt coaching with Disengaged and Effective Employees, keeping in mind that not all of the employees falling within this quadrant will be coachable. If their Immutable Laws are not matched with yours, support them in moving on!

If there are other reasons for their disengagement, coach them in addressing those issues, set clear accountability expectations and keep a tight time frame for change. If you do not see a significant improvement in their engagement within that time frame, let them go.

Remember, letting one disengaged employee go creates the opportunity for you to hire your next top performer.

This leads right to the fourth challenge rural business owners face with employees.

Challenge #4: Firing Too Slowly

When it's so challenging to find good employees and get them to come to work for you, many business owners fear firing subpar employees. Yet, in all the years I've been coaching, I have never had one business owner tell me they regret firing a subpar employee, even if they don't replace the employee right away. In fact, they all say just the opposite. Often, it takes only one firing for a business owner to recognize he needs to fire faster the next time around.

"We don't hold onto subpar employees and think, 'oh well, maybe they will turn around.' We have a lot quicker response when an employee is not a good fit. We both need to move on. We are not doing them a favor by keeping them in a job that they are obviously struggling at and don't enjoy." —Ron Parmely, Co-Owner of Overhead Door Company of Casper

Keeping bad employees can have a host of negative consequences. These people can negatively affect other employees, create issues with clients and customers, cost you business and even drive you to dislike coming to work at your own company!

Worse yet, keeping a bad employee around will get you questioning your judgment and leadership competence.

Your negative self-talk is a slippery slope: "Why did I hire that employee in the first place? How did I miss the 'red flags' in the interview? Why can't I coach this employee to be better? What's wrong with my leadership? Maybe I'm not cut out for this."

Just fire the employee and move on.

◇◇◇

"Hire slow, fire fast."

Dave Coffey, Owner of Coffey Engineering & Survey, LLC in Laramie, WY says, *"My experience in hiring fast for key positions has resulted in an employee that was misaligned with the culture of the company. There was not enough diligence in discovering if this person had the soft skills needed to fill the role. If the person doesn't gel, they will become disengaged and be a burden or even damage the company.*

For the most part, when we have hired slow it has worked out well. When we took the time to understand a potential employee's personality, work ethic, and team skills we have found an employee [who] fit well within our company, who became engaged, and performed at or above expectations. Unfortunately, it is never that cut and dry, especially when workload demands scream for help."

◇◇◇

Mike Bailey relies on his best employees to help him weed out the employees whom he needs to let go. He follows this up by increasing his expectations of his best employees, which in turn increases their engagement.

"Your best employees will help you weed out those employees that are not producing. They're the ones that have worked with them 8 hours a day.

Your best employees are going to be your best source of information for the people who are doing what they're supposed to and who are performing at the level that's up to speed with the rest of the employees. Don't be afraid to get in there and work with them and listen to them. As difficult as firing anyone is, there comes a time when you have to rip the band-aid off with all of your might. I'll guarantee you're not going to get more good employees until you get rid of the bad ones.

When you fire someone, go to your remaining employees and tell them, 'We had to let this person go. I'm going to need you all to help me get through this while we try to find more good people.' This creates a cohesive team atmosphere that helps you.

It's going to be painful at first to run short-handed, or under-staffed, or to have to train those additional people.

But what you'll find is the other employees who are still there—the good quality employees— are going to say, 'wow! Finally, they got rid of him (or her.) Now I don't have to cover that person anymore or do his job. I don't have to put up with that bad attitude.' You're going to find that the other employees will breathe a big deep sigh of relief when you terminate a bad employee."

—Mike Bailey, Bailey Enterprises, Riverton, WY

The Cost of Firing too Slowly

A bad employee can be very costly to your business.

Imagine you own a car dealership and a loyal customer walks in confused and upset to report a problem with his new car's steering.

A great employee understands the company's reputation is at stake and why the customer is upset. This employee assumes full responsibility to sort out the problem. He or she apologizes to the customer and tells him he will help rectify the problem. In the meantime, he arranges for a loaner vehicle so that the customer can go about his day. The employee apologizes for the customer's frustration and inconvenience.

Within a couple of hours, the employee calls the customer with full details about the cause of the problem and how it will be resolved. The employee even goes the extra mile (with the permission of the manager) to offer the customer a discount on future servicing of the vehicle. In every interaction, this employee is professional, tactful and resourceful.

In contrast, a marginal employee who has become disengaged likely deals with the problem differently. This employee does not feel a part of the company's success. As such, he is not willing to take responsibility or go the extra mile. In the above example, instead of listening to the customer and proactively addressing the problem, the disengaged employee might respond rudely and distance himself from the problem. The customer will leave upset and you might lose their business for good.

Imagine that scenario being repeated periodically throughout the day. Most businesses cannot afford to lose five customers a day. Rural businesses, especially, cannot afford the negative consequences of those customers talking about their experience out in the community.

Most rural business owners fire too slowly for one reason – it is challenging to find exceptional employees.

I want you to know that you will be just fine without that warm body employee. In fact, your business will be more profitable when you let that person go. There are strategies for redistributing the work among remaining employees that not only make your business healthier, but allow you to operate with fewer employees, as you attract the best employees to fill your open positions. To learn more about this, visit www.tapthepotential.com/moreprofit

DR. ANDREW SAPP, FOUNDER OF CHERRY GULCH THERAPEUTIC BOARDING SCHOOL

Lessons in Letting Go

"*Picking the right people to be involved has been wonderful because we're on the same page. They share the vision. They let me do what I do to carry out that vision. There's a level of trust there.*

It wasn't always like this, though. Some of the early partners I had hired didn't work out.

I had one person tell me she had contributed more than anybody else to the school. She questioned why I was giving her a performance improvement plan when she's so great. She did a lot, but she was micromanaging, squashing the growth of the people under her.

Another guy contributed in a lot of ways, but he claimed our success was because of him. He started sabotaging me, saying things to the other owners to decrease my credibility, trying to recruit people to work against me.

Another individual wanted us to spend an extra $3.6M on more property when we already have 220 acres. I politely said, 'You and the other owners can go ahead and do that. But I don't want to be a part of that. I don't want Cherry Gulch's money going toward that. I don't think we need more. It's too expensive and makes us less stable.'

He turned red and started yelling, 'I should just slap you…you think you know what you're doing…' Clearly he was bullying me. We would have gone bankrupt if I had chosen to make that decision.

It was difficult. I know there were times when my partners were confused as to what was really going on. They wondered, 'Is Andy the problem? Because it seems like Andy's the problem.'

Ultimately, they gained confidence in me as they saw how I handled these situations. Part of what was so difficult is some of the people I am talking about were 20 years older than I was. Now that I'm a little bit older and more established, that's less of an issue.

Although I want to do as much as I can for the staff, I'm not here for sick staff. **If there are staff who are not pulling their weight and don't catch the vision, they're a liability to me. They decrease the quality of care and the overall good that we can do. So I get rid of those people. I do it with a heart of peace, as pleasantly as possible.**

There's a time when you need to part ways with those people who become a cancer in the organization. These are not bad people that I'm talking about, but they do more harm than good.

Early on, I put up with some bad employee behaviors because I felt I needed those employees. There is a point of having the confidence to say, 'I can find some-

body else to do this...somebody who is going to have a better attitude.' That better attitude is going to invade the rest of the staff."

Dr. Andrew Sapp is founder and CEO of Cherry Gulch, a therapeutic boarding school for middle school age boys. With close to 70 employees, Cherry Gulch is the largest private employer in the county. Cherry Gulch is located in Emmett, Idaho, which is about 40 minutes from the town of Eagle (population 21,000), and about 60 minutes to Boise.

In 2010, Cherry Gulch received the Psychologically Healthy Workplace Award for Idaho. This award recognizes businesses demonstrating a commitment to employee health and well-being, while enhancing organizational performance. **Businesses receiving this award have a distinct advantage in their ability to attract and retain exceptional employees, even under difficult circumstances.**

What's Possible...

If you've been holding on to subpar employees, what's possible if you let them go?

What's possible for you?

What's possible for your business?

3

Attracting *Your* IDEAL Employees

Long gone are the days of having an employee quit, then running a classified ad to fill the position. Generic "help wanted" ads are almost useless for attracting good applicants.

First, you must acknowledge the urgency and importance of planning, networking and recruiting to fill your open positions. This must become a strategic and on-going focus in your business, with an eye toward creating a full pipeline of prospective, qualified applicants. This pipeline of qualified applicants will be your resource for future employees. You must nurture your relationships with these people, understanding this is a long-term investment. Some, but not all of your efforts, will bear fruit and pay off over time with great candidates from which to fill your open positions. The importance of this strategic initiative is equivalent to the importance you place on business development.

Second, you must come to grips with the time and effort that will be needed to adequately address this problem in your business. I recently had a business owner reach out to me due to challenges with finding and keeping employees. He told me this is an urgent and important problem, but he has very little time to devote to addressing it *(because he was so busy working in the business to cover for the shortage of employees!).* He wanted a "quick fix" and did not like hearing the harsh dose of reality I shared with him. It can be fixed, but not with just an hour or two of attention from you.

As a small business owner, you must get very smart about how you plan, network and recruit to fill open positions. **Kari Warberg Block, founder and CEO of Earth-Kind** and the SBA's 2013 North Dakota Small Business Person of the Year, is always thinking ahead, asking herself, *"What positions will I need to fill in the next 3 years?"*

Many business owners unknowingly skip crucial steps in the hiring process.[12]

Before replacing an employee or adding staff, ask:

Why are we even doing this job?

Can we do this job differently?

Can we outsource it or eliminate it all together?

Can we divide the job up among several of the people already on staff?

Can we use technology to do the job? (e.g., Voice mail and direct dial numbers have replaced duties of a receptionist.)

---

12 Mel Kleiman: 100 + 1 Tips, Tools and Techniques to Attract & Recruit Top Talent

Typically, small business owners make a decision to hire, advertise for applicants and start the selection process without enough consideration for how the position serves the business' Ideal Client and Customer, how the position will be a profit-center, and who the ideal candidate would be.

The next time you find yourself getting ready to hire, answer these questions:

How does this position serve your Ideal Customer (directly or indirectly)?

In what ways can this position be turned into a profit-center? (In other words, how can the person in this position make you money or save you money?)

Imagine you have a top performing employee in this position. What performance criteria will you hold that employee accountable to?

Now that you have taken the time to fully consider why you are hiring and how each position in your business serves your ideal client, you are ready to start finding top performing employees to fill this position.

Many business owners make a crucial and costly mistake when hiring. Rather than defining who their perfect or ideal candidate would be for a position, they hire based on choosing who is the better applicant out of the applicants who have applied. If the pool of applicants is rather small as in rural settings, this limits the qualifications. So rather than defining who is the perfect candidate for each position in their business, rural business owners let random people (applicants who happen to respond to their job openings) establish their hiring criteria.

Instead of letting applicants establish your ideal employee qualities, take the time to create your 'A-Player' descriptions.

When you know who your ideal employee is, identifying A-Players is easier. Now you know what you want. Creating job descriptions, writing advertisements for openings, and describing who you are seeking when networking will all be easier. Each step in your recruitment process will be directed to attracting your IDEAL employees.

What is an A-Player?

'A-Players' are your most valuable employees. These people have great attitudes. They always seek to work smarter. They take initiative and go the extra mile. These are the people you trust to get the job done. A-Players are good communicators who work as a team to accomplish goals. They also contribute more than other employees. [13]

Consider that any population, regardless of whether it's a rural area or metropolitan area, consists of about 10% A-Players. This means 90% of the people you encounter are B, C, D or F players. This also explains why

---

[13] Smart, Bradford (2012). *Topgrading, 3rd Edition.* Penguin.

utilizing standard hiring practices typically results in mis-hiring. The odds really are stacked against you until you acquire better strategies for finding and hiring top performing employees.

Here's the good news: **One A-Player typically does the equivalent of 9 C-Players or 12 D-Players.** It's well worth the investment of your time and energy to attract more A-Players.

Here's some more good news: A-Players tend to associate with one another. When you find one A-Player, you can tap into that person's network and get to know even more A-Players.

What is the single most important competency for an employee to be valuable to your business?

It's resourcefulness. Resourcefulness is getting over, around or through barriers to success.

Keep in mind, none of these A-Player characteristics are "trainable." This is why it is much better to structure your recruitment and hiring process to attract individuals with these A-Player qualities. You'll have much more success training skillsets.

Here are some **interview questions** that can help you ascertain how resourceful an applicant is.

When deciding how to organize your work, how do you assess what tasks need to be given priority?

Share an example of a situation in which you did not have the tools to do your job. How did you handle that situation?

When was the last time that you tried a new idea to improve your work performance and what was it?

If you were blamed for a mistake for which you were not responsible, how would you handle the situation?

What would you do if you needed to make an immediate decision, but did not have the information you needed?

While resourcefulness is a defining characteristic to look for in A-Players, you need to go a couple of steps further in defining what an A-Player is for your business. You also need to consider the candidate's goodness of fit with your Immutable Laws or your non-negotiable standards. In addition, you need to consider the personality strengths needed to carry out the duties of each position exceptionally well.

This requires some forethought before your next hire.

I'll walk you through this process. First, we start with clarifying your Immutable Laws.

Immutable Laws

What are your Immutable Laws? Immutable Laws are your core values, your fundamental, deeply held beliefs, your highest priorities and the organizing principles that guide your actions.

The challenge most of us have is that our Immutable Laws are so much a part of the fabric of who we are, that we have a hard time identifying them, much less putting them into written form to share publicly in our businesses.

We are happiest when operations in our business are in synch with our Immutable Laws. But, watch out...when one or more of our Immutable Laws is violated, we feel it. We get frustrated and angry.

One of my clients and I stumbled upon a powerful question for identifying our Immutable Laws:

What's ticked you off recently?

Think about something an employee, customer or co-owner has done recently that really got under your skin. Chances are, one of your Immutable Laws was violated. Try to put words on the Immutable Law that was violated.

For example, one business owner shared with me that he was frustrated that his employees were showing up to work "around 8:00 a.m." and often were about 5 minutes late. He had repeated discussions with them about the importance of showing up on time for work. Things would get better for a few days, but then the employees would be right back to old behaviors, strolling in a minute late, then 5 minutes late, etc.

I asked this owner what "showing up on time" means to him. His reply, "It means showing up 5 minutes early." Aha! This was an unspoken Immutable Law for him. Once he clarified this Immutable Law with his employees, his better employees began showing up early. If they were "late," they were arriving at 8:00 a.m. The owner was much happier with this pattern of behavior from his employees.

Take a few moments to brainstorm your Immutable Laws. Then, observe yourself over the coming weeks. When do you feel proud of your business? Chances are, an Immutable Law is being honored. When are you ticked off? Chances are, an Immutable Law is being violated. Capture these Immutable Laws and add them to your list.

Eventually, you will want to narrow your list of Immutable Laws to no more than 3-5 of your most important Immutable Laws. A shorter list of Immutable Laws is easily remembered by you, your employees and your customers.

Narrowing your list and getting the wording right takes some time. So, start with brainstorming your list, then try it out for a while, making changes as you go.

Here are my Immutable Laws as examples to help you get started brainstorming yours (I've been refining these for several years now):

We attract Ideal Clients and serve the heck out of them! We take care of our clients, devoting ourselves to supporting them in achieving their highest goals and being their best selves. Our Ideal Clients can count on us. We do what we say we're going to do.

Walk the talk, even when it's hard. There's no other way. Be real. Take risks. Be vulnerable.

Work hard, keep learning and have fun. Celebrate WINS and intentionally do more of what works. Being in business is tough...do the Happy Dance whenever you can!

Giving up is not an option. Persist and learn from mistakes. Mistakes are learning opportunities. Vent, learn and keep moving forward!

Work Supports Life...not the other way around. Our work is in service of the 3 Fs: Freedom, Flexibility and Fulfillment—in your business and ours.

Be a Gift from our Gifts. We seek opportunities to use our strengths to add value for our clients and our communities.

There are no 'right or wrong' Immutable Laws. Create the ones that are right for you and your business.

Only hire people whose Immutable Laws are well-matched with yours, even if that means passing up the applicant with the glowing resume because you just don't feel like they get what you are about and what you are up to in your business.

Weed out employees who don't hold your Immutable Laws. It doesn't mean they are bad people. They just don't have the same top 3-5 core values as you. Over time, you'll have a leaner, higher functioning team that you'll be proud of!

Here's another tip: Employees who share your Immutable Laws are much more likely to stick around and be loyal to your company. They will be proud to work for you. They will have your back. Isn't that what we all want from our teams?

DETECTING IMMUTABLE LAWS AND RESOURCEFULNESS IN AN INTERVIEW

Olivia Prince, owner of Wind River Realty in Riverton, WY, created a "worst case scenario" to use with applicants when interviewing.

"One of my favorite interview strategies is to use a made up scenario that our lead salesperson and I are out of town. We took a trip to Mexico. We are totally out of cell service. We have no access for you to talk to us. I have a closing coming up that you will handle for me. It's all tied up. Everything should be smooth. There shouldn't be any problems. All you're supposed to do is make sure keys and checks get where they're supposed to go. So it's not a big deal at all.

Then, the closing gets delayed. Then, for whatever reason, the staff calls in sick. Oh, man, it's just one of those days!

Now you're basically running the show by yourself. You can't get a hold of us. My clients show up at the of-

fice, freaking out. They've gone to closing and everything was fine. Then they went to the house and the owners aren't moved out. The owners won't let them in. They say that they can't let them for a couple of days. They misunderstood their contract. Their realtor hadn't been clear. Something totally crazy happened.

So they're in this U-Haul van. And they've got 3 kids and 5 dogs. And it's hotter than heck outside. What do you do? You can't call Olivia. You can't call Katie. What are you going to do to take care of this situation?

In the applicant's response, I am looking for them to be resourceful. They need to put the client first, no matter what. At this point, the applicant doesn't know any of our policies. We tell them, we know you're going to have a better idea when this really happens, but I want to know what you would come up with on your own, even though you don't know our policies yet.

I want to hear the applicant say something along the lines of, 'Oh my gosh! First of all, I'm going to bring them into the office. I'm going to let them hang out. I'm going to let them bring the dogs in, because we don't want the dogs to die of heat stroke. It's going to be chaotic, but we can't have everybody hot.

Then I'm going to try to find them a hotel or someplace to stay because they don't know anybody. I'm going to pay for that.

> *Ideally they demonstrate solving the problem as best
> as they can and they are a little creative in doing so. One
> of our main Immutable Laws is to take care of our cli-
> ents. So, I want to see that they do that in this scenario.*
>
> *If the applicant looks at me, puzzled, and says, 'Uh,
> I don't know.' That's a sign I've got a problem and it's
> probably not who I want to hire."*

Create descriptions for your Ideal Employees for the positions in your business.

Ideally, you'll want to define the Ideal Employee for each position in your company. However, this takes time and you are busy. So, keep it simple. Start with the position you intend to hire for next. Then, each time you have an open position, work through this process until you have clear descriptions of the Ideal Employee for each role in your organizational chart.

As you develop your description of your Ideal Employee for a position, ask yourself:

> *What are the results I am seeking from an employ-
> ee in this position? How will I know they are doing
> a good job?*

What personality strengths are needed to do this job exceptionally well?

How will an employee in this position demonstrate our Immutable Laws?

Some ideal qualities, such as Immutable Laws, will be universal for every employee, while others will be exclusive to the position. For instance, punctuality and a good attitude are characteristics you no doubt want in every employee, whereas being great with numbers and the ability to spot mistakes are desired qualities in bookkeepers, but may not be as important in a customer service role.

Using what you identified by answering the questions above, write a one paragraph description of your Ideal Employee for an open position.

Example: Customer Service Position

This person would be friendly, smiling, an out-of-the-box problem-solver, a good communicator and patient. He or she would have a professional attitude and a true desire to help others. This person would be punctual and a role model for other customer service employees.

With a clear description like this, anyone with whom you are talking may be able to picture someone they know who is like this.

A word of caution: As you describe your Ideal Employee for the position, stick to personality descriptors and avoid language that could be discriminatory. For example, using the word "energetic" may imply age discrimination if you hire a younger applicant after an older applicant has been turned down for the job.[14] Instead, you might describe the person you are seeking as a "motivated, go-getter" which can apply to a person of any age.

Now let's take this one step further to position you to *attract* your Ideal Employee for your current opening.

Define why your business is a great fit for your 'Ideal Employee.' Answer your Ideal Employee's unspoken question of "What's in it for me?"

What is important to your Ideal Employee?

How does your Ideal Employee stand to benefit from working for you?

What is your Unique Employment Proposition (UEP)? In other words, what makes you uniquely suited to be a great employer for your Ideal Employee?

What do you offer that your competitors don't?

Brainstorm a list of the top 5 reasons an A-Player would want to come to work for you.

---

[14] Fleischer, Charles (2009). *HR for Small Business: An Essential Guide for Managers, Human Resources Professionals and Small Business Owners.*(2nd Edition).

Here are some things to consider:

Describe the appealing aspects of the local lifestyle such as hiking, fishing, hunting, 4-wheeling, camping, low crime and so on.

Consider any perceived company weaknesses you can turn into strengths. For example, one frustrated business owner, who frequently got pulled into working in the field alongside his employees because of a lack of help, recognized he could use this to his advantage when hiring.

When he advertised for help, he positioned this as a strength that would appeal to potential applicants: *"We grew up in the business and we continue to work alongside our employees, so we know what you need to do the job and what you go through daily."*

Ask your current A-Player employees what they like most about working for your company.

Create your Ideal Employee Description before your next hire.

Once you have this description articulated, you're in a much better position to describe this person to other employees, at networking opportunities, and to write position advertisements that will stand out from your competition and attract the right applicants for the opportunity you offer.

Inoculate Your Candidates

Earlier we talked about the downside of "selling" your company to candidates. Not only should you avoid selling candidates on your company, you should be brutally honest with candidates about what it is like to work for you.

What is most difficult and frustrating about the job a successful candidate will be asked to do? Tell applicants ahead of time and let them screen themselves out before they even fill out an application. This will save you a lot of time, frustration and heartache.

◇◇

IT'S ALL PART OF THE ADVENTURE

◇◇

Jeff Warburton is co-owner of The Double H Bar, a recreational outfitting business in Jackson, Wyoming. They operate the Bar T 5 Covered Wagon Cookout where visitors ride in wagons drawn by horses for about two miles up a canyon on the edge of town. Visitors enjoy a meal and Western entertainment, including a four-piece cowboy band, Indians and mountain men.

The Double H Bar also operates the Teton Wagon Train & Horse Adventure, which is a four-day, three-night wagon train trip that crosses from one side of the Grand Teton Mountain Range to the other side. Folks ride wagons and horseback for the four days over the Tetons. They offer canoeing, horseback riding, camp activities, roping, tomahawking, knife throwing, hiking, and more.

In the winter months, the Double H Bar offers the National Elk Refuge Sleigh Rides.

This is fun work in an ideal setting—perfect for college students who flock to apply for openings. Just imagine being a college student working outside surrounded by the vistas of the Grand Teton Mountains!

However, Jeff needs A-Players who are very committed to the job, and willing to work holidays, such as Memorial Day, Fourth of July, Valentine's Day, New Year's Day, Christmas Eve and the day after Christmas. They get Sunday and another day off every week. Jeff tells people this before they even apply. But there's more he tells them...

There are aspects of the work that are not for the faint of heart. Working holidays and remaining cheerfully upbeat in frigid temperatures and harsh mountain conditions are two requirements for these jobs. Just imagine how hard it is to remain cheerfully upbeat when you are being pelted with sleet and snow in 40 mph winds.

In addition, because of the location and the nature of the work, employees live on site for the season. *"We have to find people who will be very committed to the job,"* says Jeff.

"Our employees must have great people skills. We can teach the horse skills, but we need people who can deal with other employees and the drama situations that can happen at work.

When it rains, you don't stand around saying 'I hate it when it rains.' You say, 'Wow, what an adventure!' Our attitude either helps or kills the attitude of our guests.

Many of our guests are here one day. If we say, 'Oh, man, I wish you'd have come yesterday. It was so much better. The weather was better. The experience was better. It wasn't as dusty. It wasn't as whatever. You can find something wrong with anything if you look hard enough.

But if that's our attitude, we can't expect our guests to walk away saying, 'That was cool!' It doesn't work that way. So we need people who can adapt and work through any sort of challenge that comes up. We need people with attitudes of, 'This is all just part of the adventure!'

So if it's a little dusty today, say, 'Aren't you lucky, because this is part of the adventure.' Or if it rains, say 'It's raining today. You're lucky. This is part of the adventure.' How we deal with the conditions will be how our guests deal with it. If an employee gets depressed when it rains, then they pass this attitude on to our visitors."

So, what is it about working for you, and doing what you will ask your employees to do, that is hard, difficult, or challenging? Ask your best employees. Let them know you want to attract more employees, who like them, are more than willing to work through the hardest parts of the job.

When you have completed the description for your ideal

candidate for a position, use your requirements in your job advertisements and interviews to help people either disqualify themselves or commit to your standards.

Getting a flu shot bolsters your body's ability to fight the flu. Similarly, inoculating your applicants by letting them know about the hardest parts of the job greatly increases the likelihood they will deal with these challenges with minimal complaint. Your best employees will be proud of the challenges they overcome in working for you!

Now that you have greater clarity on who is an A-Player for your business, it's time to find these people. Yes, they exist, and you may be closer to hiring them than you realize!

What's Possible...

What's possible when you're hiring A-Players?

Just imagine...

What's possible for you?

What's possible for your business?

4

Where to Find *Your* A-Players

"Hire people who are better than you are, then leave them to get on with it. Look for people who will aim for the remarkable, who will not settle for the routine."
- David Ogilvy, The Father of Advertising

You really want to hire the best, but where do you find them?

On average, about 10% of the population is comprised of A-Players. If you live in a rural area, with a population of 7500, you can expect that 10%, or 750 of your fellow citizens will be A-Players. However, of that 750 people, some will be children, some will be elderly and some will have a disability that prevents them from working. What's more, you can expect that almost ALL able-bodied A-Players desiring employment will be employed. THIS is why it is so darn hard to hire A-Players! But, it's not impossible. It just takes some strategy and focused attention on your part. Remember, it's well worth your effort!

Just like you need to "always be marketing" for your business to succeed, you need to "always be networking" with A-Players to keep a pool of applicants available for your future openings.

If you fail to do this, you will be limited to the applicants who just happen to respond to your advertisements at any given time. Broaden your search! You greatly increase your odds of hiring A-Players at any given skill-level when you intentionally network with A-Players.

The 'A-Player' Network

In all likelihood, you already have at least a few A-players in your business. Skeptical? Come on now, at least one of your employees (i.e., YOU!) is an A-Player.

Your best employees hold the clues to finding more A-Players.[15] To find more A-Players, get to know your best employees better. Discover and tap into their networks.

If you are the only A-Player you can identify in your business, start there. Tap into YOUR networks. You know other A-Players. Think about the groups to which you belong: professional organizations, the Chamber of Commerce, Kiwanis, Rotary, your church, your neighborhood association, or your kids' baseball team, etc. These are just some of the many networks of which you are a part.

You're probably thinking, *"But, Sabrina, they have jobs. They aren't interested in working for me."* Maybe…or maybe

---

[15] Smart, Bradford (2012). *Topgrading, 3rd Edition.* Penguin.

not. You'll never know if you assume they can't help you fill your openings. Even if they aren't interested, chances are, they may know someone who would be interested.

If you have done your homework to describe your Ideal Employee, you can easily describe the type of person you are seeking. You can ask if they know of anyone like that. Even if the person they know is currently employed, you can ask that they put you in touch with that person so you introduce yourself. That person may seek you out in the future. What's more, that person may know another A-Player who is looking for exactly what you offer. This is the **chaining effect** that happens with effective networking.

You want to take advantage of "chaining" when you are networking to connect with A-Players. Never consider one contact a dead end. Get in the habit of asking, *"Who do you know who might be interested in an opportunity like the one we are offering?"*

If your small town is anything like ours, the "gossip chain" is highly efficient, and you cringe when you or one of your employees is the source of this week's negative gossip. Put the gossip chain to work for you in a positive direction. Get the A-Players you know, telling the A-Players they know, about the opportunity to work with you. You, an *Employer of Choice* in your small town, are growing again.

Back to your best employees. They are a goldmine for finding other great employees. It's time to get to know them better. What you learn will offer clues to finding more employees like them. Plus, the added benefit of this effort is that your employees will be honored that you care enough to want to get to know them better and that you want their input.

Here are some questions to get you started in getting to know your best employees better:

When you first applied, how did you hear about us and the open position? (These answers provide clues to referral sources and places to advertise for future applicants).

Why did you come to work for us? (These answers are clues to what would make it attractive for an A-Player to work for you versus another employer).

What do you like most about your job and about our company? (More clues for what makes your business attractive to A-Players).

What clubs and community organizations do you belong to? (Pay attention—this is where to start networking and recruiting. HINT: Get your employees involved in community organizations and let them recruit for you!)

What social media sites do you use? (Discover where A-Players are connecting. Show up there and add value to their network by sharing helpful tips, resources and educational content pertaining to the interests of your A-Players.)

Who are the A-Players you know? (Keep in mind, these people are likely employed and are not seeking work right now. However, they may be seeking better opportunities. Connect with them. Build a relationship. Add value in their world so they come to see you as an Employer of Choice within their circle.)

The next time you have a job opening, recruit from your network of A-players. A-Players know more A-Players.

As a general rule of thumb, **A-Players 'hang' together** in their social circles. With a bit of innovation and organization, you'll become more effective in recruiting the best employees.

How to Attract A-Players

You can greatly increase your chances of finding and attracting great employees by adopting strategies within your recruitment process to make your business attractive to A-players.

Make your business an Ideal Place to Work for Your Ideal Employee

You should know why every A-Player who has worked for you accepted your offer. Why did they choose to work at your business?

Similarly, anytime an A-Player leaves your business, find out why. Don't be afraid to ask this question. You need to know what you can do to improve your chances of keeping A-Players.

◇◇

Charisa Fox and her sister of Fox Family Cleaning in North Dakota compete for employees with the high paying oil fields and other competition in an area with a labor shortage. Yet, they hire and keep help. All of their current employees have been with her for over a year.

I asked Charisa what she is doing to get and keep A-Players.

"I think it's because we are family-oriented. We don't just treat our family like family; we treat our help like family and we pay well.

Employees want to feel appreciated. Be up front, keep a real relationship, reward them and discipline them when the time is right. It's kind of a balancing act. Sometimes you have to keep things in check.

You always need to show appreciation and put yourself at their level sometimes. I never have them do any-

thing that I haven't done. Anything I ask them to do, I can do just as good or even better.

I think the appreciation builds because my employees know that I can come in and show them anything. I'm capable of doing what they do.

As a small company I often know my employees a little better than a larger business. If my employees are having problems or hard times, I help. Maybe something is wrong with their car and they need an advance. If they are a single parent and something is wrong with their kids, maybe there is something I can do to help. If there's anything that I can help with, I do. I know everybody and their personalities. If they're going through hard times, they know they can ask me for help.

I have to remember what makes me an employer that they would want to stay with rather than going somewhere else. You have to ask, 'What can I do?' and 'How can I make them feel they don't want to leave?"

Become an 'Employer of Choice'

A-Players are not just looking for any job. They are looking for a career. The 4 most important qualities A-Players seek from an employer are:

1. A great boss and co-workers. If you have a large percentage of A-Players working for you, flaunt it! Similarly, if you know why your employees like working for you, share this with prospective employees.

2. Interesting work

3. Growth and opportunity to advance their careers

4. Work-life balance

If you offer any or all of these, build this into your recruiting messages.

A-Players are motivated by the opportunity to move up in your business and advance their careers. **Small businesses in small towns are uniquely positioned to offer advancement opportunities to A-Players.**

A-Players like the idea of being able to move into higher level positions more quickly in small business than in the corporate world and bigger cities.

They like the breadth of the work they get to do in a small business, rather than being confined to a narrow role. They WANT more responsibility and feel good when they can be competent in successfully fulfilling your expectations of them.

Small businesses are much better positioned than larger organizations to meet the work-life balance needs of their employees. Why? Small business owners can flexibly address work-life balance with their employees. Larger organizations tend to take a "one-size" fits all approach to this issue, which is very frustrating for employees. According to Stewart Friedman, professor of Management and the founding director of the Wharton School's Leadership

WHERE TO FIND YOUR A-PLAYERS

Program, "It's not an uncommon problem in many HR areas where, for the sake of equality, there's a standard policy that is implemented in a way that is universally applicable – [even though] – everyone's life is different and everyone needs different things *in terms of how to integrate the pieces. It's got to be customized.*[16]"

As a rural business owner, you have an opportunity to shine as an employer of choice in your community. Get to know the unique needs of your employees and work with them to balance their performance at work with other areas of their life that are important to them.

Many of the successful rural business owners I interview are doing just that, but not in a formal way. It's just who they are. They care about their employees and work with their employees when various circumstances arise in the lives of their employees. If this is something you are already doing, it's time to "toot your own horn" and make it more widely known that this is a benefit of working for you.

◇◇◇

Mike Bailey of Bailey Enterprises shares what he is doing to help his employees with work-life balance:
"We try to create an environment where we're flexible enough that we can work with people's schedules to

---

[16] John Keyser. Are We Happy Yet: How coaching is improving workplace morale. Choice Volume 11, Number 4. pp 19-20. December 2013

a point. We still need people to come to work every day, but we've got people who share daycare with each other. We have one lady who works evenings and one lady who works mornings. They watch each other's kids sometimes. This helps us gain those employees who maybe wouldn't be here if we weren't that flexible.

Our business is not a 9-5 kind of business. We're open 24/7. We have early and late shifts. Plus it can be really challenging to find employees who will work weekends and holidays. But they are out there.

We've got employees whose spouse works a certain time of day, so the employee needs to work a different time of day to take turns with their spouse watching the kids.

There are lots of families out there with multiple income earners. That's part of what we have to work around. We're flexible, helping people find solutions to some of those issues we all have in our lives."

Make time for conversations with your employees to find out what matters to them. This goes a long way toward creating a culture where employees feel connected, appreciated, and supported in thriving in all areas of their lives.

Discover YOUR Pool of Ideal Employees

Did you know the opportunity to work for you is the answer to somebody's prayers?

It may surprise you to learn there is a pool of your Ideal Employees just waiting for the opportunity to work for you. They just don't know about you yet.

Just who are these people and where do they hang out? That is what you need to figure out.

Who needs the opportunity you are offering? Even more importantly, what groups of people need the opportunity you are offering? Beyond that, where do these people gather? In other words, *what are the "congregation points" for these individuals who are potentially Ideal Employees for you?*

This is much easier to determine once you have thought through the qualities you are looking for in an employee.

Let me share an example to illustrate this concept. One business owner in the construction industry found himself in a real pinch a couple of years ago. He needed employees to fulfill his contracts, but the applicants just were not showing up. He was facing a lot of competition from the oil field and it was not at all unusual for a recent hire to show up for work for a week or two then just disappear after taking a higher paying job in the oil field. In a pinch, this owner hired a couple of his wife's friends to fill positions in his crews.

As I worked with this business owner, he came to see that a solution he perceived as a simple effort to solve a problem in a pinch, might actually be developed into a long-term solution that would allow him to expand his business.

As it turned out, the female employees stayed with his company longer, were more reliable on a day-to-day basis and were more conscientious in maintaining his equipment. When he placed them on crews with male employees, those crews worked more efficiently than the all-male crews. Although there were some duties the female employees could not carry out due to the physical requirements, when placed on crews with male employees, their male counterparts were able to complete those tasks.

Through our work together, my client decided he would speak with these female employees and find out what they liked about working for him. They were earning higher wages than they had in previous retail and restaurant positions. He already knew this, but something else he discovered through these conversations really surprised him. The seasonal nature of the work was an "intangible perk" for these women.

Up to this point, my client had perceived the seasonal nature of his business as a liability because he could not offer his employees year-round full-time employment. These women told him they actually appreciated the seasonal nature of the work because it allowed them to work hard a few months out of the year to add to the family income, but still be available for after school activities and other family obligations during much of the year. For these women, the opportunity my client provided was an answer to their prayers.

My client decided he could fill a couple more open positions with female employees. He asked his female employees if they had friends who might be a good fit for the company.

Sure enough, one of the women had two friends who had been stay-at-home moms, but now that their children were in school, they were looking to get back to work. Neither of these women wanted to work full-time, but both were very excited to learn of the opportunity to earn a high wage working full-time 4-5 months out of the year. After they were hired, both confided in my client that working for him really was an ideal solution to bringing more income into their household while still being available for family commitments much of the year. One even commented, "It's the perfect balance!"

With each hire, my client is becoming more well-known as an employer of choice among this network of mothers of school-aged children. He has utilized this network to not only hire more female employees, but also to fill other positions on his construction crew. Just recently he immediately filled an open position by hiring the husband of one his female employee's friends.

By thinking outside the box, my client was able to tap into an extensive network to fill his open positions. He identified one commonality—that they all have school-age children and want to contribute to their household income in a significant way, but do not want to work full-time.

These mothers do not "congregate" at tradeshows or club meetings. Their "congregation points" are more informal. His female employees are connected to one another through sports events, after school activities and social media. My client does not participate in these school activities or sports events, so he never encountered these women. Instead, he asked his best employees if they have friends who would be a good fit with the company.

The more curious my client became to understand the particular needs of his best employees, the more he became aware that he provides an ideal solution to their desire to contribute to the family income without working full-time year round.

Every business has a different culture and offers different opportunities for its employees. Discovering YOUR pool of Ideal Employees starts by getting to know your best employees and why they like working for you.

Innovative Solutions to Labor Shortage

Rural business owners are resourceful! When we are faced with a challenge, we find solutions.

Kari Warberg Block, founder and CEO of Earth-Kind, had a big problem on her hands. She needed employees to grow.

Headquartered in Bismarck, North Dakota, Earth-Kind has the mission to "preserve the good and prevent the rest," by providing proactive, natural alternatives to protect the spaces in which we live, work and play from pests and odors. Earth-Kind is best known for Fresh Cab Botanical Rodent Repellent product, the first and only natural repellent product to meet Federal EPA Standards for both safety and efficacy.

Kari and her company have received multiple business awards. Kari is second runner-up for the 2013 National Small Business Person of the Year Award by the U.S. Small Business Administration and is the SBA's 2013 North Dakota Small Business Person of the Year.

"We got started in 1995 as a farmer's market business. I had small kids and we lived on a farm. I wanted to be there to raise my kids and wanted to do a business that would supplement our income. I also wanted to do something that I felt improved humanity.

Over the years our business grew. I started with just myself and later added 4 full time employees—still working from the kitchen table. Today we have about 45 employees. We do business throughout all of the United States and Canada. We innovated in the retail market as the first all natural pest control.

Our roots are still very rural. In fact, my title is 'Farmer in Charge'. That's what my employees call me. Part of that is due to our culture—our real roots—the way that I believe our business runs and should be run. To me, it's very much like farming. I consider culture to be our rich organic soil because it's our people that make things work.

Initially, we moved the location from the farm into town, because I was paying my employees to drive 45 minutes to work. That was one of the benefits we offered to get good people. The commute added 45 minutes to their day. So I paid for their time, plus I paid them for their miles.

After I added it all up, I realized it would be more cost effective to rent something in town.

Then the oil field moved in. That caused a housing shortage. I actually had employees living in my house at one time! That became unmanageable.

We relocated our plant to the Minneapolis area, south of the city, again in a rural community that had a very similar culture to what we had grown the business with. Then we moved our corporate office location into Bismarck, ND.

When we were struggling due to the labor shortage in a rural area, one of my employees said, "Have you ever thought of hiring the handicapped? They show up every day. They love their jobs. They never get sick."

We've actually built our whole plant around these employees—even the equipment—so they can grow things. A lot of these individuals have been able to get out on their own because of the confidence and skills that they've gained in working for us.

We have 12 full-time developmentally disabled employees. They love the consistency of doing the repetitive things that might bore other people. It also gives them the opportunity be part of a community, which is extremely rewarding for them.

So that's how it started, and we've never looked back.

They've been fantastic.

There are a lot of plusses on our side. This let us grow debt free by utilizing labor, instead of equipment.

We've also found it's a wonderful morale booster. People feel really good working when they know that somebody next to them is very happy in their job. It lifts up everyone.

They pray for us. Their families are supportive. It's just wonderful.

They do work slowly, but here's the deal…they are consistent. They are stable. And when you figure in all of that, plus what it does for the morale, it's amazing.

They've solved some pretty big problems for us too. They see things we don't. One day I walked in and they said, 'How come you don't sign this?' I said, 'What?' They said, 'How come you don't sign your label with your name? Aren't you proud of it?'

I said, 'You know, that's really cool!' So I started signing all my labels, like putting my stamp on it."

Mark and Linda Hunter of Hunter's Furniture & Appliance in Afton, Wyoming also tapped into an overlooked labor pool to fill a key position.

"Several years ago we had a close friend sell his business after 35 years. His last day was a Saturday and his first day with us was the following Monday. He was 62

years old and a little broken down after running a very successful tire and auto repair shop. But what he lacked physically, he made up for in so many overlooked areas. He understood work ethic, he was a natural in customer service, he was punctual, and he was careful in operating our equipment and vehicles. He was not addicted to a cell phone and was very steady and paced himself. He understood when to use grease and when to use a hammer. He worked for us for 4 years until he had to have both knees replaced. Our warehouse was fairly new and when he left, it still looked new.

This employee's replacement was a thirty year old man who had one way of doing things – 'fast and hard'. We incurred damage to our equipment, warehouse, furniture and appliances several times per week. His speed killed our profit. I have learned that a steady, slow pace can be so much more profitable!

Don't overlook the retired who have very desirable qualities. Best of all, they need something to do!"

Attracting & Keeping the Best Employees for Your Entry-Level Positions

Many small business owners find it difficult to fill entry-level positions. There is a lot of competition for labor for unskilled positions and that can often leave small business owners feeling pressured to compete with wages paid by larger employers in their area. When you are maxing out on the wages you can afford to pay an entry-level employee and still remain profitable, it's time to consider other perks.

Small businesses have a KEY advantage over corporate employers, but very few owners recognize it, much less leverage it. The advantage is this: a great employee has the opportunity to advance their career much more rapidly in a small business than they ever could in a larger corporation.

Many businesses advertise the "opportunity for advancement." Yet, very few small business owners give much thought to what this really means. Even fewer have articulated a clear path of advancement from an entry-level position through the ranks of the company.

Keep in mind, the best employees are interested in advancing their career. **You are at risk of losing your best employees when they are unclear as to how they can advance their careers with your small business.**

The next time you are hiring an entry-level employee, here are some questions to consider:

What is the next promotion for this employee?

What is the pay increase for that promotion?

What criteria must that employee meet to receive a promotion?

What personality strengths are needed to perform the duties of that next position exceptionally well?

What skills are needed?

Will you provide the training needed to acquire those skills? If not, how will you support that employee in acquiring the necessary training?

Keep asking yourself this same set of questions for each promotion as an entry-level employee advances in your company. Once you have answered these questions, you are in the position to tell an applicant about real career opportunities with you.

Consider the difference between telling an applicant, "We start you at $10/hour and you have the opportunity to advance with us" versus telling an applicant, "We start you at $10/hour and if you work hard, over the course of the next 5-10 years, we'll support you in moving up into a management-level position, with the opportunity to earn $60,000 or more annually." The second scenario will be much more attractive to a career-minded applicant, making it more likely you will attract and retain an A-Player employee for your entry-level position.

TIP: Make the first promotion easily achievable for an employee who is a real go-getter. This is psychologically motivating and will increase your odds of retaining that employee over time.

Employee Referral Incentive Programs

If you have an employee who is actively talking to others about how great it is to work for you, reward that, even if they have yet to hand over an applicant. In other words, reward the behavior you want the employee to repeat.

Get your current employees motivated to recruit for you by offering them a reward for any new hire they refer.

Employees who come from referrals stay longer because they already know someone on the job. They know what they are getting into because their friend described the job and working conditions to them beforehand.

Educate your employees about who is an Ideal Employee for the positions you want to fill.

Ask A-Player employees who else they know who they would consider to be an A-Player (at former jobs, from clubs and organizations they are in, etc).

Here are a couple of pointers about employee referral incentive systems:

- Customize the incentives you give based on the preferences of the employee making the recommendation. One employee may value a day off to spend with their kids in the summer, whereas another employee may like a gym membership. These incentives don't have to cost you a lot; just zero in on what your employees like.

- Give the incentive upon the actual hire of the new employee.

- To increase your likelihood of retaining A-Players, give the referring employee an incentive on anniversary dates of the other employee.

Let's look at an example of how an Employee Referral Incentive Program might work. Your employee, Joe, recommended Tim to work for you. Tim turns out to be a real A-Player. You hire Tim and give Joe a gift certificate to take his wife to dinner at a fancy restaurant on Valentine's Day. You did this because Joe is a newlywed. Joe is thrilled! You've made him look really good in his new wife's eyes.

Six months go by and Tim is rocking and rolling. He's now fully trained and doing the work of four employees whom you let go because they had been doing just enough to get by and made a lot of mistakes. You drop a note in Joe's box telling him how thrilled you are with Tim, thanking him again for bringing Tim to the company.

Joe reads the note and checks in with Tim. Joe is now very invested in making sure his buddy Tim is happy with working for you. Plus, Joe likes working with Tim. Joe was fed up with those other four employees who always created more work for him. With Tim on board, Joe's life at work has been a lot easier!

Another 6 months go by. Tim has been with you for a year. Plus, with your employee referral incentive program, he has recommended two more A-Players whom you have hired. You are kicking back, pleased with yourself that in one year's time, you've let four really bad employees go and replaced them with three A-Players. Your profits have doubled because you have been able to go after 3 times the amount of work you had in the year prior and are generating a lot more revenue—with fewer employees! What's more, since you cut the slackers from your team, costs have gone down considerably (they had been making a lot of costly mistakes, requiring considerable re-work).

You reflect on all of this and decide you want to do something really nice for Joe. After all, Joe helped you get the ball rolling in the right direction by recommending Tim to you. You've noticed Joe looking at travel magazines on his breaks. You ask him about that. Turns out, he wants to take his wife away for a nice weekend for their anniversary. This gives you an idea. You surprise Joe with a weekend getaway at the mountain lodge a few hours from town. This costs you less than $500 because it's the off-season. Joe is thrilled. He feels extravagantly well taken care of by you. You consider this gift a nominal token of appreciation. After all, your profits have doubled in the last year!

Joe now sings your praises to everyone he encounters. Tim and his buddies do the same because they've all benefitted from the Employee Referral Incentive Program. You have great applicants chomping at the bit to come to work for you. But, you are selective. You only hire the best.

Employee Referral Incentive Programs are easy to implement and produce quick results. If you are in need of employees right now, I recommend you start with this recruiting strategy. I've seen it work time and again. It's a great strategy to quickly fill open positions with very good employees.

Expand Your Referral Program

Expand your referral program beyond employees. Consider offering incentives to friends, family, former employees, vendors, etc. The more people you let into your referral program, the greater your reach and the better chance you have of getting the best employees.

Often Overlooked Sources for Employee Referrals[17]

- Call former A-Players who left you and ask them for referrals. Maybe they've met A-Players since leaving your business. Who knows? Maybe they are not happy in their new job and would like to come back to work for you.

- Consider A-Player employees who have retired, as well as those who left their job with you to go to school or raise children. They may want to work part-time to fill in while you fill the open position, or they may know someone to refer to you.

---

[17] *100 + 1 Top Tips, Tools & Techniques to Attract & Recruit Top Talent* by Mel Kleiman.

- Don't forget to consider your customers. Let them know about position openings. Your best customers can be great referral sources. Who knows? One of your best customers may want to work for you!

You get the idea...tap into all of your networks to get more qualified applicants for a position. Call anyone you know who may know someone like the person you are seeking to hire. The more specific you are in describing the personal qualities you are seeking, the more likely you are to trigger the person you are talking to think of someone they know.

For example, instead of saying "I am looking to hire a receptionist. Do you know of anyone looking for work?", you might say: "I'm looking to fill a receptionist position. I'd like to hire someone who is warm and friendly, who is great at putting people at ease and who pays attention to the little things that matter. Does anyone come to mind?"

Remember, A-Players are hardly ever out of work. So, if you ask someone in your network who they know who is looking for work, their A-Player connections may not come to mind.

Getting Employees Involved in the Community is a PLUS for Your Business

Anytime your employees are out and about in your community, they are conducting public relations for your business. They are interacting with people who may be future employees for you.

Educate your employees to properly represent and promote your business in the community. Exceptional employees want to work for enterprises with professional reputations.

Encourage your A-Players to be involved in the community so they get to meet more A-Players. This is especially important for employees who have moved into the area to work for you. You want to help them establish deep, strong roots in your community. They are much more likely to stay! The additional benefit of doing this is that your employees build their networks of A-Players.

When employees come to work at Teton Therapy, owner Jeff McMenamy makes it his business to help them build their connections in the community, particularly if they have recently moved to the area.

"I help my employees make connections in their areas of interest. For example, one of our employees said she was really into diving and loved coaching, so I immediately put her in touch with the local high school athletic director.

She became the diving coach at the high school. Now she is more deeply involved in the community doing something outside of work that she is passionate about.

I also make it easy for my employees to meet people.

For example, I introduce them to people in my circles that have common interests or similar life stages.

I also emphasize the importance of my employees' behavior in the community outside the workplace. I talk to them about how we need to treat people with respect and be courteous even in the event of conflict. In a small community everyone will know who you are and where you work."

Mike Bailey, President of Bailey Enterprises shares, *"We invested in a really nice uniform for our employees to help our employees feel they are part of the overall enterprise and raise our visibility with our customers. Our employees are very easily recognizable in the community. Your employees leave work, they go out into the community, they're going home after work in their uniform, or stopping off at the store in their uniform. They're representing your business. People are watching them working or walking down the grocery store aisle. We are in a real small town where people know each other.*

Many of the people they run into are going to be current or future customers, or future employees."

◇◇

Take this a step further by turning your employees into recruiters for you while they are out and about in the community.

Equip your employees with a business card that they can give to A-Players they encounter. In addition, to the employee's contact information, include your direct contact information. On the back, include a few bullet points about what makes you an 'Employer of Choice' for A-Players working for you.

◇◇

Mike Bailey likes to acknowledge good service with the card he hands out in the community. He puts the following on the back of his business card:

I noticed you doing a great job! Are you looking for new opportunities? We've been looking for you...
- Competitive Wages
- Simple IRA
- Vacation/Sick Days
- Advancement Opportunities
- Drug FREE work environment
- Insurance; medical, dental, optical

"Every time I go to a restaurant, a fast food joint or a grocery store, and I see somebody giving good service… an upbeat, positive employee, I'll hand them my card and say, 'We're always looking for good people.' At a minimum you're giving that person a pat on the back and telling them they're doing a good job. Let's face it, none of us do that enough.

When one of my employees does this in the community, it makes more of an impression. It has way more value coming from an employee of the company than it does coming from me as the owner. If an employee is saying, 'Hey, this is a great place to work; we'd like to have you here' that means a ton to them. It has way more value than me telling them that, because they think I might just be blowing smoke and complimenting them because I want more employees, which I do. But, I'm also not going to hand these cards to people I don't think would be good employees."

Chuck Parmely of Overhead Door Company of Riverton-Lander gives a business card to his employees to share in the community. This is what is on the back of the card:

GREAT
JOB!!!!

THIS CARD COULD CHANGE YOUR LIFE!

At Overhead Door Company we notice people like you!

The person giving you this card thinks you could be a good fit for our team.

You may not want to change jobs right now, but who knows what the

future holds. Just hang on to this card. When you are seriously thinking of

a change, come by and see me.

Work with Schools

Think long-term when you are filling your pipeline of A-Players. Develop a relationship with your local college or trade school. Teach continuing education courses or volunteer as a guest speaker in classes with students who will eventually have the skills you are seeking. Make your contact information available for students. Stick around after class and chat with the students. Collect contact information from any who impress you. Stay in touch! Although you may not hire this person immediately, you are building a network of A-Players. Who knows? That student may be a future employee for you or they may refer a friend or family member to work for you.

You can also create intern opportunities for students to establish relationships and assess their possibilities as potential future employees.

This is an excellent strategy for filling professional positions, especially when you are bringing in talent from out of state.

◇◇

Jeff McMenamy of Teton Therapy has established clinical affiliations with physical therapy schools.

We 'audition' students, so to speak, through a 3-month internship program. We promote these clinical affiliations by traveling to the schools. Most of the students have no idea what Wyoming is about. The biggest barrier is that they do not have a place to stay once they get here. Many say they would love to come for three months, but they don't know anybody with whom they can live. Financially, they're broke college students, so they can't afford to go get a hotel or anything. We've addressed this by providing affordable housing.

When they're here with us as students, we make sure they have a really good experience. We try to get them involved. If they don't know anybody here, we try to offer them activities on the weekends and introduce them to local activities they might be interested in, such as hiking or fishing. If they like skiing, we try to schedule their internship in the snow season. I rally the rest of the team for an activity they are interested in and then include them so they feel like they are part of the team. They get to know us and experience Wyoming.

And then if we like them, we can say, 'Maybe you want to think about taking a job with us later.'

Student Loan Repayment Programs

Some professions benefit from student loan repayment programs. Teachers, social workers, physical therapists, nurse practitioners, psychologists and physicians are just a few of the professions that may be eligible for student loan repayment in exchange for a commitment to serve in an underserved area (i.e., RURAL area!)

In fact, this is how I came to move to Riverton, WY from Austin, TX upon completing my doctoral degree. As a psychologist working in an underserved area for a two-year commitment, the National Health Service Corps paid off my student loans. When you consider the interest that compounds on those loans over the years, it was like winning the lottery!

Check into state and national loan repayment programs for the professionals you hire. You might be pleasantly surprised to discover a strong perk for recruiting that doesn't cost you anything!

Acquisitions & Downsizing

Do you know of any businesses in your area that are going through a merger, acquisition or downsizing? Employees in those businesses are typically very stressed by the changes happening, particularly if it's a hometown business being acquired by an outside corporation. They fear losing their ability to serve their customers in the friendly, community-oriented way they've enjoyed. Corporate policy often tramples over small town values. This is a prime time to network with A-Players in these businesses and let them know about the opportunities you offer. This is the time to emphasize job stability and your roots in the community. Who knows? You might pick up a few new employees.

Work with Other Businesses

Develop cooperative relationships with other local business owners who have similar Immutable Laws as you. When you have openings ask if they have any great applicants they did not hire. Reciprocate when you receive applications from 'A-Players' you do not hire.

This is a particularly good option for businesses with seasonal needs for employees. If you can identify a business that has a peak season opposite of yours, you may be able to share employees. This is a Win-Win-Win situation. You are developing a strong relationship with a fellow business owner who can send business your way and vice versa. Plus, your employees can be employed year-round. They will appreciate not having to scramble for work in the off-season. Plus, you are less likely to lose them to another employer when they find work in the off-season.

Get Seasonal Help Coming Back Over & Over

If you use seasonal help, give the A-Players a partial bonus for signing on for the next season before the end of this season. Give them the remainder of the bonus a few weeks into the next season.

Use your seasonal people when regular employees are on vacation or you have sudden increased demand from customers.

Send Your Employees on the Road to Recruit for You

When you send your employees to conferences or trade-shows, remind them to be on the lookout for A-Players. Send them with a stack of your referral cards.

Ask your employees to come back with names and contact information for at least 3 or 4 people who could possibly be great employees for you. If you have an Employee Referral Incentive Program, your employees will be more than happy to do this.

When the employees come back, follow-up quickly with any contacts they made.

Introduce yourself immediately with a short handwritten note. Mention the name of the employee who mentioned them to you. Consider including a brief article, tip or resource that could benefit the other person.

Don't forget to stay in touch with these referrals, so be sure to add them to your database.

Publicize Your 'A-Players'

Feature your 'A-Players' in your company newsletter and the local papers. Run a column or advertisement in the newspaper where you focus on your best people, where they came from, how they got their jobs, why they stay and why they love their jobs. Your customers will love getting to know your employees and this puts a human face on your business.

Have you promoted from within? Send out a press release. Build your reputation as an employer who provides opportunities for community members to advance their careers by staying local.

The added benefit: A-Players are reading! You will be piquing their interest in working for you.

Help the Family

When you are recruiting an A-Player who will be moving into your area, you must address the needs, concerns and hesitations of their spouse and children. A move to a new town is a significant life stressor.

Many a rural business owner has lamented to me about the problems "importing" talent into their business. If you don't address the fears and concerns of the spouse and children, your applicant may disappear. Or worse, the employee starts working for you, only to leave 6 months later because their spouse couldn't find work or their children had a hard time adjusting.

When a new 'A-Player' employee is moving from out of town, help their spouse find work. Also, find out their interests and help the family get integrated into the community.

'A-Players' hang together; the spouse of your new A-Player employee is likely to be an A-Player. Helping the spouse find work makes it likely your 'A-Player' will stick around.

Helping a fellow local business owner by bringing a potential A-Player applicant to their attention is a Win-Win-Win! They may return the favor in the future.

Plan for Labor Needs

Planning for how much help you need and how much you need to pay will help you attract 'A-Players.

When Charisa Fox of Fox Family Cleaning bid for new work, she considered the competitive wages in each area needed to attract employees.

"We pay competitive wages. So we bid our contracts out according to what we had to pay for those competitive wages out there. People were not settling for less than about $15 an hour for service jobs," tells Charisa.

Find Their Hot Buttons

What's important to your prospective employees? Find out what matters to them and show them how working for you will help them achieve these things.

Jeff McMenamy was living in Wisconsin when he was recruited by an employer in Wyoming.

"What really made up my mind is what happened when I took off a day from work. My wife, our two children and I took our camper and boat, and went to this lake in Wisconsin.

When we got there, they told us that they were booked out about a month in advance, even though there was hardly anyone there. Apparently everyone shows up later on Fridays. I thought, 'This is crazy. I can't even go camping. You have to plan a camping trip a month in advance just to find a campsite?!'

Our whole weekend was wrecked and it was so foreign to me because I had moved from Montana. I had lived a lifestyle where I could just drop everything and go do something outdoors. I couldn't do that in Wisconsin.

Then I got this call from somebody in Wyoming asking me to come out for an interview. They paid for my airline ticket, meals and hotel. All expenses were paid. The guy who interviewed me had worked with me before in Montana, so we knew each other. He knew exactly what my interests were and what buttons to push. We did spend a little bit of time at the facility, but he knew that the job wasn't necessarily what would convince me to move here—it was the lifestyle. He took me through Sinks Canyon. I asked, 'Where are all the people?' I saw these lakes, all these open campsites and nobody around. It was just so different from what I was dealing with in Wisconsin where people from Chicago would just flood these areas on the weekends. He played *on what was important to me.*

This guy also knew that I had two young children. When I said I wasn't interested in the job, he said, 'Let me talk to your wife. I want to offer something to her.'

He asked her, 'What would it be worth to you if you could stay home and raise the kids?' That was something we had never even considered. We couldn't raise two kids on one income in Wisconsin. He told us that in Wyoming you can make a great living due to the lower cost of living and lower taxes.

So immediately, he touched on two very important buttons to us. One was the opportunity for my wife to stay home. I would have done most anything including working a crappy job for that. Then he had showed me this beautiful outdoor area. I was sold.

I now do the same when I recruit. The last doctor of physical therapy I hired was from Chicago. He was also very interested in the outdoors, so I drove him to the mountains and across the Continental Divide. That was very powerful for him.

I asked him, 'Outside of work, what other things do you do in your life? What do you do when you're not at work?' That's probably one of the biggest questions, and I typically do not ask that as an interview question. I'm just really interested in the person. I want to find out more about them, When I am with potential hires, I want to find out what interests they have that might align with my interests, or someone on my staff.

During our phone conversation, this PhD candidate told me he wanted nightlife and restaurants. I wasn't going to lie to him. I said, 'There is a little bit of nightlife and a few restaurants, and I'd be happy to show you those, but if that's a big priority on your list, let's save the trip here to visit.'

He said the outdoors was at the top of his list. So I said, 'Okay, then that would be the right reason to come out and we should move forward.

Then I dug deeper and asked what he liked about nightlife and restaurants. He responded, 'It's really important that I have a place to go meet people and make friends or go hang out with friends.'

So I drew from my own experience in the rural setting and told him, 'When you are looking for those kinds of similar activities or looking for friends and so forth, there are fewer people here, but the connections you build with them will be much deeper around here.

You'll find a common thread with people and your outdoor interests whether it's rock climbing, hiking, fly fishing, hunting or whatever. You will find some people who are really passionate about the same things that you enjoy. Those are some of the people you are going to make some really good, deep connections with.'

When he came aboard, I introduced him to many people and took him to places where he could meet people, because he's so good at being social and he loves that.

Don't Forget to Stay in Touch!

We've covered a lot of strategies to connect with A-Players. It all comes down to building a chain of connections with A-Players and staying in touch. After all, it does no good to do all of this networking if you don't stay in touch. Your contacts go cold and the next time you have an open position, you'll be right back where you started—filling the position based on who responds to your ad at the local job service office.

Start a database of good quality people you encounter, who you would consider hiring. Create ways to stay in touch. Send holiday cards, birthday cards, articles, newspaper clippings, etc. Stay top of mind.

If you have a company newsletter, keep former employees on your mailing list. This is a great way to gently remind them of the opportunities you offer, why you are an Employer of Choice in your area and to mention your Employee Referral Incentive Program, so they can continue to refer to you long after they've moved on.

Connect with A-Players you know via LinkedIn. LinkedIn gives you the opportunity to not only see who A-Players are connected with, but you can also discover their professional groups, giving you another avenue to explore for A-Players.

Also, ask your best employees what social media platforms they use most. It would be good to have a presence on those sites to help you stay top of mind in their networks.

This is just a sampling of the strategies that work to find great employees in rural areas. What I've shared here are the strategies that are working in every industry. There are many more strategies you could employ.

At Tap the Potential, we help our clients identify the simplest, most effective and profitable strategies for their individual needs. The key is to identify what works for your business, then systemize it so you have a steady stream of qualified candidates inquiring about working for you—an Employer of Choice.

What's Possible….

Just imagine…

What's possible when you're hiring the best employees?
What's possible for you?
What's possible for your business?

If you've read all the way to the end, you're clearly committed to overcoming the challenge of attracting top performing employees to your business. I acknowledge you for your commitment! It will certainly pay off.

I want to extend a special opportunity to you to apply for a private Profit Maximizer Consultation with us ($497 value). In the Profit Maximizer Consultation, we will uncover your best opportunities to transform your business into a highly profitable, *Great Place to Work* so that you become an Employer of Choice in your community.

Employee problems are often an area where money leaks out of the business. We'll discuss your specific employee challenges, and identify the most relevant strategies to overcome the challenges you're experiencing. To submit your application, go to: **www.profitgift.com**

Bibliography

Carr, Patrick & Kefalas, Maria (2009). Hollowing Out the Middle: The Rural Brain Drain and What it Means for America. Beacon Press.

Fleischer, Charles (2009). HR for Small Business: An Essential Guide for Managers, Human Resources Professionals and Small Business Owners (2nd Edition).

Gillham, Christina. Doughnut hole country. Newsweek. October 29, 2009.

Keyser, John. Are we happy yet: How coaching is improving workplace morale. Choice Volume 11, Number 4, pp 19-20.

Kienast, Theresa A. Engage employees and become a superhero! Choice, Volume 10, Number 2.

Kleiman, Mel (2010). 100 + 1 Top Tips, Tools & Techniques to Attract & Recruit Top Talent.

Lipman, Victor. Why are so many employees disengaged? Forbes on-line. January 18, 2013.

Pryce-Jones, Jessica. Positive profits: How happiness at work impacts the bottom-line. Choice, Volume 11, Number 4, pp 27-28.

Smart, Bradford (2012). Topgrading, 3rd Edition. Penguin.

About the Author

The Business Psychologist™, Dr. Sabrina Starling specializes in transforming rural businesses into highly profitable, *Great Places to Work.*

Dr. Starling recognizes that **employee problems can be one of the biggest stumbling blocks for any business owner.** With her background in psychology, and years of driving profit in small businesses, Dr. Starling knows what it takes to find, keep and get exceptional performance out of your biggest investment—your employees.

Access Dr. Starling's comprehensive video training *5 Secrets to Exceptional Employee Performance* (her gift to you!) at **www.tapthepotential.com**

Contact Information

Dr. Sabrina Starling
Tap the Potential LLC
P.O. Box 13596
Alexandria, LA 71315
Visit our website: www.tapthepotential.com

sabrina@tapthepotential.com
(800) 975-9440 ext. 725

Twitter: @drsabrina
LinkedIn: www.linkedin.com/in/drsabrina